VERDE VALLEY LORE

As Published in

The Times of Fountain Hills

L.J. Schuster Company
7707 East Acoma Drive, Suite 102
Scottsdale, Arizona 85260

Other books by the Author:
Kansas Farm Boy
Our Desert Oasis

Library of Congress Catalog Card Number: 97 93667

ISBN 0-9659937-0-1

Verde Valley Lore as published in
The Times of Fountain Hills

Copyright 1997 Robert Mason

Cover art by Maree Lee Eger

Map by Elaine Waterstrat

Published by:
Robert Mason
18529 Horseshoe Bend
Rio Verde, Arizona 85263

CONTENTS

Preface i
Introduction ii
It Happened Here iii
Photo Credits iv

Azatlan---Arizona's Capitol? 1
Prehistoric Mysteries 4
Metate Quarry 9
1000 Years Ago 12
Verde Valley Geology 16
Red Mountain's Gunsight 20
Desert Harvest 24
Carlos Montezuma, M.D 27
Gen. Irvin McDowell 31
Old McDowell Had A Farm 35
Stoneman Military Road 39
Dreams Shattered On The Verde 45
The Two Faces of Capt. Chaffee 51
Maryville--Our Ghost Town 56
McDowell/Reno Military Road 62
Al Sieber--Arizona's First "Scoutmaster" 70
Tom Horn---Good Guy or Bad? 75
Box Bar Ranch 80
The P-Bar Ranch 85
Verde Cattle and Cattlemen 90
Sheep and Their Bridges 96
The Rio Verde Canal 103

Almost A Lake--The Orme Dam	107
Cool, Clear Water	113
Two Rivers Run By Us	116
Our "Dammed" Rivers	120
Granite Reef Dam	124
Supervisor Jim Hart	130
That Evening Glow is "Tuff"	134
Phon Sutton and Coon Bluff	137
Purple Mountain Majesties	140
Postscript	147
Bibliography	148
Index	149

PREFACE

I have known Bob Mason for many years. Our time together is always well-spent reminiscing about this area of the American Southwest that is so rich in history. For the past several years, he has been a regular columnist in our newspaper, and we constantly receive comments from readers as to how enjoyable his stories are. His copy is well-documented, and his interest in researching topics is quite evident in his very readable copy.

As you read the following pages, you will find his commentaries most interesting as he takes you from the banks of the Verde River where 800-year-old Hohokam Indian artifacts have been found, to the slopes of the McDowell Mountains where he gives you an insight into the area's geological makeup to taking a journey down the Stoneman Military Road.

Enjoy yourself.

Alan Cruikshank, Publisher
The Times of Fountain Hills
Fountain Hills, Arizona

INTRODUCTION

Researching the history of the lower Verde Valley has been like peeling an artichoke. Each layer has been a story to be uncovered and there always seems to be another absorbing topic that emerges.

When the idea of a *Times* column was suggested by Alan Cruikshank, it seemed likely that 8 or 10 efforts would exhaust the subject matter, this author and, more worrisome, the *Times* readers. Happily, the first two concerns have not occurred. The third seems to be constructive but all votes have not been counted.

Initially, time for the interviews and journeys to research locations had to be found after golf, bridge and tennis. More recently, the reverse has been true, thanks to the competent staff persons and the array of resources in the Luhrs Reading Room and the Arizona Historical Foundation, both at the Hayden Library. The Phoenix, Mesa and Fountain Hills library personnel have also been enormously helpful. Salt River Project people and the Tonto National Forest staff in the Phoenix, Mesa and Cave Creek offices have contributed by helping sort through fact and fiction.

Duplicate bridge partner, Mac McConville, helped rescue some errant, dangling participles and find the right places for those pesky commas. The most help of all came from my wife, Dorothy, and daughter, Marty, who have been my careful proofreaders and my most honest counselors. Dorothy says she has forgiven me for the hundreds of uncommunicative hours spent huddled over the word processor.

These stories may be read in any order. Each began as a column and stands on its own as a chapter. Hopefully, this book will serve as a reference document that enhances your appreciation of this fascinating part of Arizona.

Robert Mason

IT HAPPENED HERE

PHOTO CREDITS

	Page(s)
Todd Bostwick -- Pueblo Grande Museum	10
Bob Fedden	19,21,30,89, 130,131
Jim Marshall	21
Arizona Historical Foundation	53,72,100
Arizona Collection	28
Robert Mason	28,43,50,60,65, 68,74,139
Matthew Brady	31,41
Orwell, Ohio *Star-Beacon*	52
University of Wyoming	77
Julie Hoff	67
Alan Cruikshank	88
Tonto National Forest	101
Fay Schlotfeldt	102
Salt River Project	109,121,123, 128
Max Esssex	114
Todd Photography	122,141
Maricopa County	133
Phon Sutton Jr.	138

AZATLAN---ARIZONA'S CAPITOL?

Most Arizona residents probably are unfamiliar with the name, Azatlan, yet a location with this name exists adjacent to the communities of Fountain Hills, Rio Verde and Tonto Verde. To understand its origins, we must go back 135 years when the western portion of the New Mexico Territory was split off and called the Arizona Territory. Almost immediately controversy developed concerning the site of the territorial capitol.

Two sites had their advocates for capitol status. The largest town at that time was Tucson, whose recorded history dates to 1775 when a Spanish presidio was established there. Prescott was in contention because of newly-established Fort Whipple and the early gold discoveries in the Bradshaw Mountains which had attracted a significant population.

A third contender was apparently the first choice of many. Marshall Trimble, in his book, *Roadside History of Arizona*, relates how early territorial leaders, led by Lt. Colonel Francisco Chavez, set out from Zuni, New Mexico in 1863. They intended to establish a capitol city near the junction of the Salt and Verde rivers. This spot was favored since it would be a "neutral" location between the two established, rival towns of Tucson and Prescott.

The site at the mouth of the Verde was to be called Azatlan, an Aztec name said to be their mythical place of origin. It has also been identified as a region in northwestern Mexico, where they were apparently living at the time of the Spanish conquest. The word is sometimes written as Aztlan. On July 25, 1866, this name was also applied to the first Masonic Lodge in Arizona, opened in an upper room of the old log capitol building in Prescott.

The Chavez party tried to follow the Verde down to its mouth, but they were blocked by rough terrain (probably south of today's Camp Verde) and never achieved their goal.

By Oct. 1864, the site selection was still not made but the legislature was leaning toward Prescott. Tucson's close ties to the Confederacy while the Civil War was still in progress was a severe negative. The Tucson delegation was jealous of the honor about to be bestowed on the fledgling village of Prescott so they vowed to support "anything else."

When the bill designating Prescott as the capitol was to be voted on, amendments to move the site to La Paz and then the lower Hassayampa River were introduced by the Tucson group and failed. They then offered language that stated, "...to a point within ten miles of the junction of the Rio Verde with the Salado....and that said permanent seat of government shall be called Azatlan."

This was also defeated, but by the narrowest of margins. Had the death of a Tucson delegate not occurred and had one of the western delegates switched his vote, the history of this river confluence would have been vastly different.

The name, Azatlan, has emerged, phoenix-like, to be applied to a large archaeological site just north of the Ft. McDowell reservation boundary and on the west bank of the Verde. It is estimated that several thousand persons lived in this area at its peak, which probably occurred between 1100 and 1350 AD.

Charles Poston, an explorer, miner and statesman, who has been called the "father of Arizona," visited this area in 1861 and wrote of finding... "the remains of three large Indian villages just above the confluence of the Verde and Salt Rivers." He described this portion of the Verde as a "wild, weird area." He was no doubt

Azatlan - Arizona's Capitol

referring to the heavy vegetation, the threat of Apache raids and the abundant evidence of ancient civilizations.

The Azatlan site has been professionally excavated in 1956 and again in 1964. Archaeologist Philip Schnering said, "This site has the greatest concentration of worked stone I have ever seen." He is referring to the large amounts of basalt and other stones that were chipped and otherwise shaped by the Indians for their tools.

It is clear that the lower Verde Valley communities live on the edge of a fascinating piece of history--and prehistory!

PREHISTORIC MYSTERIES

Artists, for centuries, have painted their versions of landscapes and events to provide useful insights into the past. Later, the written word and the printing press allowed a more precise record. We now possess even more accurate methods of documenting events for future generations with cameras, records, discs and tapes.

How can we learn about those civilizations that existed in the Verde Valley before any of these methods were available here? We see traces of their presence but the very definition of "prehistoric" tells us that there is no readily available record of their culture. In spite of this, we have learned much about these ancient inhabitants of our valley. How is this possible?

Archaeologists study the remnants of these people and are able to form a remarkably complete set of conclusions. This is accomplished through the study of information that can be classified as:

1. Features
2. Artifacts
3. Ecofacts

FEATURES

These are identified as a human alteration in the Earth's topography and as being attached to or a part of the ground. Examples of features are:

<u>Habitation Sites</u>

In our area these are generally pit houses dug into the ground two to four feet, walled and covered with poles, limbs and brush. The size, shape and density of these sites tell the experts much about family and social configuration.

At Casa Grande this feature manifested itself in a multi-story adobe building and at Mesa Verde as cliff houses.

<u>Rock Walls</u>

These are not widely used in our area since the naturally occurring stones do not easily lend themselves to this purpose. They are common to the north, both in the construction of dwelling sites and as protective or defensive structures.

<u>Trash Mounds</u>

These features are also called "middens." They were the garbage dumps of 1000 years ago and, like today's landfills, they provide layer upon layer of life-style evidence. Often this stratification is helpful in dating a site. Many mounds are still evident here and although eroded, for the trained observer they answer many questions.

<u>Roasting Pits</u>

Conical holes were dug in the ground from 3 to 5 feet deep and about the same diameter at the top. They were used for cooking agave hearts, the carbohydrate staple of the Hohokam diet.

Later, after irrigation, corn and beans were probably parched in the same pits.

Post Holes

During pit house excavation, it is possible to learn the pattern of roof and wall supports based on the post hole positions. Occasionally a preserved post will provide a tree-ring dating or a burned post a carbon-dating sample.

Hearths

These were small fire pits generally used inside each pit house but sometimes just outside. They are well defined and can often provide an archeo-magnetic sample.

Iron particles in the soil align themselves magnetically when the soil in the hearth is first heated. The magnetic pole has moved through the centuries in a pattern that is well known to scientists. Thus, the position of the magnetic pole at the time of the first usage of the hearth can be determined within about 50 years.

Canals and Check Dams

These features are most often eroded or altered by later usage. Any water control device can show the extent and style of irrigation techniques and give an indication of the productive capacity of a given area.

Ball Courts

These are generally oval depressions associated with prehistoric villages of larger size. Many experts feel they are a cultural extension of the elaborate stone courts of central Mexico and Yucatan. It is speculated that they were also used for dances and ceremonial or community events.

Cremation Sites

The Hohokam commonly practiced cremation and interred the remains in ceremonial pots, sometimes with ornate, prized possessions accompanying the burial. Whenever such a site is found the appropriate Indian authorities must be notified and they decide the disposition of the remains.

Petroglyphs

These are patterns incised on stones that usually, but not always, were covered with a desert varnish patina which allows greater contrast. The inscriptions have been interpreted in many ways. They may have been religious expressions, clan symbols or a form of communication. Perhaps they were simply an artistic statement or a precursor of today's graffiti. They do provide a haunting, and somehow more personal, glimpse of these ancient people.

ARTIFACTS

These cultural items are those whose physical properties have been altered by human activity and have been transported from their original, natural location.

Pottery sherds

Professionals use this spelling (not shards). These are also called "ceramics" and are numerically the most commonly occurring evidence left by our area's prehistoric inhabitants. They were made from the two most readily available materials, soil (clay) and water, with small amounts of "temper," such as sand or mica, to strengthen the finished, fired product. Much can be learned by careful analysis of sherds, especially decorated items and those containing a portion of the vessel rim.

Lithics

This is a word of Greek origin used to describe any stone altered by human endeavor. A great variety of tools were fashioned from an igneous stone called aphanitic basalt. This stone is very dense due to slow cooling and can be split into fragments with naturally sharp edges.

Rapidly cooled lava usually forms vesicular basalt, a porous rock containing many holes and widely used for grinding stones.

River rock and other ground stones were used as hammers, anvils, choppers and axes.

Exotics

In this context, the term means items traded into an area. The presence of trade goods confirms contact with other tribes and the production of materials in our valley that were desired by others. It is likely that some ceramics, tools and foodstuffs from here were traded for obsidian, chert and flint that were used as projectile points. Turquoise from northern Arizona and New Mexico, copper bells from Mexico and shell from the Pacific and the Sea of Cortez are also found.

ECOFACTS

This term is applied to naturally occurring specimens that can shed light on life styles. Examples would be pollen, seeds and various kinds of animal bones. The incidence of this category is limited but can be significant in some situations.

****

From the various features, artifacts and ecofacts, scientists can form relatively accurate inferences about family size, population, life span, general health, diet, amount of conflict, agricultural practices, time of occupation and social structures.

By learning more about ancient civilizations we can reconstruct not only what happened in the past but we are able to deduce something about the general laws of cultural history and the rate of changes in a given environment. A hypothesis can be tested by tracing it to the present. If it can be found to have a good correlation, a projection can be made and used as a predictor of future cultural changes.

The rich archaeological sites in the Verde Valley have been crucial to the study of the Hohokam people. They may also help us relate this to our own pasts--and future.

METATE QUARRY

At the Scottsdale-Fountain Hills boundary there is a site that was once the scene of frequent and intense prehistoric Indian activity. This location had nothing to do with the activities that are most commonly investigated by archaeologists. It did not involve a habitation, a ceremonial location or a hunting spot. This significant discovery has been identified as a metate quarry.

Metate is an Aztec word used to describe the lower unit of a two-part grinding stone. The early varieties of corn and the seeds of many desert plants including jojoba, mesquite, palo verde and ironwood possess a very hard exterior surface and require processing for human consumption.

Pounding creates a splattering of the seed parts and significant loss of material. The most efficient method found by prehistoric people was to grind the grain between two stones, the metate and a hand-held tool, called the mano.

Basalt is the stone formed by cooled lava extruded as a result of volcanic activity. If the molten material cools rapidly, it hardens before all of the air escapes and the resulting stone is filled with many holes. This is called vesicular basalt which is ideal for a grinding surface. As the stone erodes, the air holes continue to emerge and provide sharp, cutting edges.

Although there are many suitable sizes, a typical metate would be about 14 inches wide and 20 inches long. It might begin as a 6-inch thick piece of stone and, with use, become basin-shaped, ultimately being eroded beyond further use.

The large item is a metate. Grain or seeds are placed on the stone and ground with the hand-held mano. Perhaps this is where the expression "Between a rock and a hard place" originated!

Scattered on the desert floor around the lower Verde Valley are many pieces of metates, some worn away, but it was also the custom of many tribes to break or hide their grinding stones before traveling to a new location. It has been theorized that this was to prevent other tribes from finding a ready-to-use tool. It simply may have been a practical decision that it was easier to find and shape a metate in the new location than to carry it.

The wearing-away of the mano and metate created a negative side effect that was probably not understood by the prehistoric people. Their chief food source was ground seeds and grain. As the volcanic stone in the manos and metates slowly eroded with grinding, the resulting meal contained particles of pumice. This diet gradually eroded their teeth, a fact noticed by archaeologists as they uncover skeletal remains. Persons identified as being in their 20's, based on other characteristics of their skeleton, had teeth that were more worn than those of a 70-year-old today.

There are some classic deposits of basalt along Shea Blvd. just east of the Mayo Clinic entrance. They are on either side of

Metate Quarry

Shea but are most dramatic on the south side--especially the two small peaks known as Saddleback Mountain. Just west of this formation is a ridge, also on the south side of Shea, containing large quantities of vesicular basalt that has cracked into blocks, many of which are roughly 1 to 3 feet square. Archaeologists have identified many places where slabs have been split off for metates and manos. This was generally accomplished by using dense greenstone or river cobblestones as hammers to obtain chunks which were then shaped into metate size by pecking and flaking. The site has several locations where the ground is covered with basalt flakes, the result of the quarrying process. Some rudimentary stone circles also exist, probably representing structures of some kind.

Vesicular basalt also exists in large quantities on the east side of the Verde north of Fountain Hills but these deposits are not as accessible and generally not as uniformly fractured as at the Saddleback Mountain site.

Todd Bostwick, archaeologist for the city of Phoenix, discovered this site several years ago. His 1993 published report says: "It is one of the two major Hohokam ground stone quarries in the Salt River Valley. The other is along New River, near the Westwing Mountains. It is likely that the Hohokam people traveled many miles to 'harvest' their grinding stones at these locations. Metates and manos from these quarries have been identified at every habitation site in the Salt River Valley."

Shea Homes has recently built Carino Canyon Homes just south of this quarry. Access to the ridge is limited but the next time you're driving in that area take a look at the lava deposits just west of Saddleback Mountain and remember their place in the prehistory of our area.

1000 YEARS AGO

We know that the lower Verde Valley has many advantages that attract a growing number of residents. Less well known is the fact that 1000 years ago this area was one of the main population centers in the Southwest.

In recent years we have watched archaeologists at work along the Beeline Highway just east of the Verde River bridge and from Gilbert to McDowell prior to widening of the road. Other work has been done along Bush Highway and on the Ft. McDowell Reservation. Have you wondered what they were finding? Summaries of recent excavations tell a compelling story of this area 10 centuries ago.

Prehistoric people began to arrive here around 100 BC. They were nomadic, following streams as they moved to places of greatest natural food sources. Their diet was uncertain and life expectancy was short. About 300 AD they began irrigating crops.

As corn, beans and squash were successfully grown, nutrition improved and the nomadic, hunter-gatherer life style became more sedentary. Life spans increased, with rapid population growth. About 500 AD, some decorated pottery began to be used, primarily on ceremonial vessels and specialized objects such as scoops and effigies. This denotes an allocation of more time to pottery making, an indication of less time needed to hunt and gather food.

Let's take a brief look at six of these sites:

WATER USERS
(Archaeological Consulting Services, Tempe)

This location was at the present tubing parking lot on the Salt River just below Stewart Mountain dam. Seasonal occupation likely began around 500 AD. There was only one feature that showed some communal organization...a pit house group around a courtyard dated to the late Colonial period or 800-1000 AD. In this configuration each of two or more pit house doorways face a common activity area. This village likely did not exceed 100 persons at its peak. Occupation ended about 1050 AD. There is some evidence of a withdrawal about this time to the lower Salt, Verde and Gila valleys.

Pollen samples show wide use of plant resources, most of them native to the Salt valley. An interesting exception is jojoba (ho-**ho**-ba) residue since it does not grow in the immediate area. A corollary finding was the discovery of pottery that was made at the Azatlan site on the Verde north of Fountain Hills. This shows that there was trade between these communities located 16 miles apart. Evidence of turquoise from the north and marine shell with Pacific coast origins widen this trade circle.

Stone tools were primarily of the food processing type, basalt manos and metates for grinding grains and seed. Many well-shaped projectile points were also found as were basalt knives and scrapers. Stone pendants, clay figurines and shell ornaments were present.

BLUE POINT BRIDGE
(Scientific Archaeological Services, Phoenix)

Artifacts here were similar to Water Users, except that the materials used for the making of pottery were different even though the locations were only 2 miles apart. In each case they used the clays available nearby. One ballcourt was here, a sign of a larger, more organized village.

FT. McDOWELL RESERVATION ROAD
(Archaeological Consulting Services, Tempe)

Occupation here continued until about 1300 AD. Pottery and other trade materials were found that originated with the Sinagua from the north and the Salado to the east. More and larger stone tools were here, linking these people with the Azatlan site and with more extensive agave processing. Projectile points were fewer here than at the Water Users site.

BEELINE HIGHWAY AT VERDE BRIDGE
(Northland Research, Flagstaff)

This site was initially called "La Escuela Cuba" for the Cuba School located here in the early 1900's. It showed habitation as early as 100 AD continuing until about 500 AD. It was then abandoned for about 200 years.

The next occupation showed a more organized system with some pit houses in courtyard groupings. These people used large ditches for irrigation of crops. Their pottery was of somewhat lower quality. Major floods about 900 AD and in the mid-1300's likely ruined the canals several times and probably contributed to abandonment around 1400.

One of the larger canals here was cleared and rebuilt in this century. It was called the Velasco Ditch for Benjamin Velasco, a lessee of the Ft. McDowell farm in the 1880's. A modern commentary on this ditch noted that in 30 years of use, it was partially destroyed and rebuilt 4 times. This underscores the challenges faced by the Hohokam as they struggled to maintain their extensive system of irrigation canals, diversion dams and headgates---all constructed by hand and with naturally occurring materials.

LOWER BEELINE
(Northland Research, Flagstaff)

These excavations were between Gilbert and McDowell and on the north side of the old highway in most cases. Initially, this site was similar to other Salt River settlements. During the later occupation, divergence has been noted with intrusions of cultures from the north and east.

Like the Pueblo Grande location near Sky Harbor Airport, this site was at the upper end of irrigation ditches serving the valley north of the Salt. These people may have been very influential in the control of water for a wide area. After 1150 AD, their habitation patterns shifted from pit-houses to at least some free-standing adobe structures. The villages here were larger and in later years platform mounds may have replaced ballcourts for what is believed to be ceremonial and recreation purposes. Canal destruction from floods also occurred here and the villages were vacant after about 1450 AD.

TONTO VERDE
(Soil Systems, Inc., Phoenix)

This location, just north of Rio Verde, was a part of the large Azatlan site. It was excavated in late 1991. Nine areas were opened, with 5 identified as being seasonal activity places. Two "farmsteads" were found with dwelling sites that were probably occupied for many generations. One contained three pithouses clustered around a courtyard in the classic Hohokam style.

Another spot, called a "village," revealed many activities; roasting pits, cremation burials, tool manufacture and a wide variety of pottery sherds but strangely, no habitation sites were uncovered.

Some well-decorated artifacts were found, notably a scoop with a bird-head effigy as its handle, a shell mosaic pattern on a possible mace or prayer stick, and a decorated paint palette with traces of red pigment still visible on it. Occupation here was at its peak from 900-1100 AD, though usage probably continued until 1350 or 1400 AD.

****

Each site has a different story to tell. They yield their ancient secrets slowly---and only to the careful observer. Bit by bit, the clues emerge and the mystery is less elusive. These people deserve our admiration for being able to scratch an existence from the desert and create a relatively well-organized culture. It's remarkable that after 1000 years the trained scientist can still find clues that increase our knowledge of this resourceful civilization.

VERDE VALLEY GEOLOGY

About 2 billion years ago, the area that is now the lower Verde valley was at the bottom of a large sea. About one billion years later there was a large amount of volcanic activity. The oldest rocks now visible here, the McDowell Mountains, were formed during this Pre-Cambrian era. They are largely a combination of schist, granite and diorite, much of which cooled slowly underground.

This was a time of violent weather. For millions of years, torrential rainstorms, earthquakes and volcanic upheavals occurred. Soil particles and fragments were swept from high ground, building sedimentary layers on the ocean floor that would accumulate to a thickness of hundreds of feet. After deep burial these sediments were changed to stone by heat and pressure.

As the leveling process continued, these rocks were eroded to relatively flat surfaces about 600 million years ago. At this time Arizona was intermittently covered with shallow seas which retreated from time to time as the area was uplifted.

Verde Valley Geology

Less than 100 million years ago this location became dry land. Upheavals formed larger mountains and lower valleys. This era is known as the Laramide mountain building stage. Geologic processes have since created the basin and range pattern characteristic of our area.

As land surfaces were exposed, different life forms came into being. The former sea beds, with their rich layers of sediment and crustacean remains, nourished plant, bird and animal life in abundance. During this time mammoths, saber-toothed tigers, and giant sloths were present.

This was a plateau although it was certainly far from level. Its elevation was such that the present Verde Valley drainage actually ran to the **north!** Laramide-era rocks from here have been found in several locations on the Mogollon Plateau. Only about 5-8 million years ago did the Colorado Plateau begin its steady uplifting process, finally reversing the Verde River flow. This same uplifting allowed the beginning of the erosion process that created the Grand Canyon.

At this time the Verde was many miles wide and several hundred feet deep. Enormous amounts of sedimentary and conglomerate rock were deposited in random locations in our area. Lousley Hill, just seven miles north of Fountain Hills, is the best example. Geologists have noted that it contains a larger variety of stones with origins outside this area than any other formation in the lower Verde valley. The Needle Rock formation 14 miles north of Fountain Hills is a part of a ridge that is composed of the remnants of rock deposited by this ancient river. On both sides of the Verde there are numerous river rock deposits, sometimes quite deep and well above the present river level--evidence of the size, depth and power of the stream.

During this time the McDowells were eroding, building talus slopes on either side of their northwest/southeast orientation. Over the millions of years, this range has lost about 4,000 feet of its height, with the debris creating the long slope to the Verde. As the valley gradually filled from the west, the river was slowly pushed against the more rugged, and geologically more complex Mazatzal Mountains (properly "Ma-**zat**-sal" but commonly "**Mat**-a-zal"). Core-drilled samples reported by Clifford Pope, Jr. in his ASU thesis, *Geology of the Lower Verde Valley*, show sand and decomposed granite debris from the McDowells to a depth of over 1000 feet in some spots west of the river.

The Laramide era also caused huge sand deposits to be laid down just south of Fountain Hills. The sandstone that formed Mt. McDowell, commonly known as Red Mountain, and the Papago Buttes, was probably deposited about 40 million years ago. Iron in the sand has oxidized to create its distinctive color. Basin and range faulting and erosion have occurred since then, exposing these massive sandstone beds.

Other significant mountain ranges are visible to the southeast----first the Usery Mountains, then slightly east, the Goldfields with their vertical, west-facing cliffs that provide such spectacular views in the late afternoon.

On the far southeast horizon, the Superstitions provide a hint of the mystery and intrigue that has surrounded them for more than 100 years. This tortured wilderness was formed about 25 million years ago during an intensive, localized period of volcanic activity. Following these mighty upheavals, the extruded material collapsed back into the cavities formed during the eruptions. The resulting chaotic mass of rocks is called a "caldera." The complex ruggedness of the Superstitions is better understood when the origin is identified.

A landmark in the Superstitions is Weaver's Needle, often thought to be the plug or neck of one of these extinct volcanoes. However, it is simply composed of harder igneous rock than the surrounding area and therefore has resisted erosion.

Another distinctive feature of our landscape is Four Peaks which is largely formed of granitic rocks uplifted into a harder quartzite and diorite formation. These cap rocks are erosion-resistant and thus have protected the rest of the formation, preserving much of the elevation created by the original uplift.

A good example of nearby volcanic activity are the lava flows that are evident on Shea Blvd. as we go west into Scottsdale.

Saddleback Mountain, on the south side of Shea around 140th St., is the best example but there are others. These deposits are interlayered with the sedimentary rocks deposited after the uplifting of the mountains. On Shea Blvd. some dramatic igneous intrusions, or dikes, can be seen in the cuts on the north side, just west of the Eagle Mountain entrance.

Molten lava was squeezed into a crack in the sedimentary layers. Intense heat has oxidized (burned) the adjacent stone.

Bob Brooke, a professional geologist living at Rio Verde, helped with this topic. He says, "The geologic history of this immediate area provides a fascinating, complicated, and dramatically scenic record of the processes forming our planet."

RED MOUNTAIN'S GUNSIGHT

There are many landmarks on the Fountain Hills horizon but few are more unusual than the gunsight. This dramatic slot in Red Mountain has prompted many discussions and undoubtedly lots of looking and pointing as we show guests and newcomers our desert scene. What created this unique bit of geology? Let's take a vicarious hike to this spot and learn more about it.

About 80 million years ago, massive geologic processes caused an uplifting of the bedrock granite. This was accomplished unevenly, creating mountain ranges and basins between and below them. The resulting terrain was sharply defined.

Erosion then began smoothing this harsh environment, a process that continues even today. The bedrock was altered by plant life and eroded into the basins adjacent to every set of uplifted mountains. These erosion products were deposited in layers which gradually accumulated in some places to a depth of many hundreds of feet. As these layers were compressed by the pressure of material above them they became stone. The contents of this sedimentary fill was primarily sandstone conglomerate with inclusions of many boulders of granite and quartzite that did not erode into sand but simply washed into the basin intact.

Red Mountain's Gunsight

About 30 million years ago, volcanic materials would periodically intrude into seams of this fill and lava flows would cover portions of the terrain.

Enormous weight transfers occurred as a result of the erosion process and about 10 million years ago the Red Mountain portion of the basin was tilted and uplifted. As this happened, vertical fractures were created. Millions of years of erosion have again softened the landscape, separating some of the sandstone bluffs and buttes into columns.

The rocks that make up Red Mountain are not seen on the surface at many places in this region. They are thought to be about the same age and composition as the head of the camel of Camelback Mountain and the Papago Buttes.

The presence of black lava flows and red sandstone create a contrasting scene as a hiker begins the trip. The terrain is so uneven that soon after leaving the Beeline Highway the associated sights and sounds of civilization fall away. In some of the arroyos and rockfalls one can easily imagine that the hike is occurring in a remote wilderness area.

The last part of the climb to the gunsight is difficult and treacherous. There are thick stands of jumping cholla and loose rock on the slopes of the mountain. Chartreuse-colored lichen covers many of the sandstone boulders, adding another dimension to the rugged terrain.

*This dramatic scene captures the attention of
Beeline Highway travelers and Fountain Hills residents.*

The gunsight is a nearly vertical fracture that has been widened by wind and water erosion, creating the feature that enhances our skyline. The base of the slot is at an elevation of 2140 feet and the width at that point is 15 feet. This latter figure was surprising for it appears wider when viewed at a distance. The width narrows a few feet above the base and does not widen until near the top where tilting has caused the western portion of the ridge to fall away.

The vertical measurement of the opening is estimated to be about 100 feet on the east and 80 feet on the west. There is very limited level space at the bottom of the gap----the floor slopes sharply away to the north and south.

In the slot another vertical fracture can be seen that extends into the east face of the mountain more than 30 feet and extends from the base to the top. At this point there are many quartzite and granite boulders in the sandstone that are up to 2 feet in diameter. As erosion occurs, the harder boulders protrude and eventually pop out during freezing and thawing or heavy rainstorms. This gives the fracture the appearance of an environment in transition. Fresh, rounded cavities are evident where rocks recently dropped from the rock face. A pack rat had made his home in one of these.

As would be expected, the view is spectacular. Granite Reef Dam is directly to the south. At nearly the same spot the Central Arizona Project Canal dips under the Salt River, then is pumped up to start another downstream portion of its journey to Tucson. To the north, all of Fountain Hills and the McDowell Mountains dominate the scene. The radar dome on Humboldt Mountain 31 air miles to the north-northwest is visible, as is McDowell Mountain Park, Rio Verde and Tonto Verde.

The correct geographic name for Red Mountain is Mount McDowell and it is considered to be the southeastern end of the McDowell Mountains even though its sandstone and conglomerate are geologically different. The rest of the McDowells are granitic and metamorphic in origin.

The trip to the gunsight is not recommended because of the steep, unsafe climb, but for those who have always wondered about this distinctive landmark perhaps these facts will help answer questions and enhance your appreciation of this unique topographical feature. Bob Brooke, a Rio Verde resident and retired geologist, made the journey with the author on two occasions and helped with this report.

DESERT HARVEST

It's a desert out there--and for many Arizona newcomers, it can be intimidating. However, for the prehistoric people who lived here, it was a preferred site.

The casual observer sees cacti and a profusion of thorny shrubs and trees. To the Native Americans, these were welcome, life-sustaining elements. When the dependable flows of the Salt and Verde Rivers were combined with the productive soil, this became a favored area.

Most of us would guess that the Hohokam lived mostly on wild game---rabbits, deer, bear, fish, birds and rodents. However, archaeological evidence shows that plant foods constituted a majority of their calorie intake. Meat was a delicacy, savored only on occasions when the hunt was successful and even more infrequently as tribes became more sedentary, depleting wildlife in their immediate area. For some tribes in Arizona, fish was not a part of their diet.

The mesquite tree was the most widespread and important resource for the native people of the Southwest. Various parts were used for food, fuel, shelter, weapons, tools, fiber, dye and medicine. The harvest began early in the summer, making this a time of plenty since many trees continue to produce for several months. The pods themselves were used as a carbohydrate source and were traditionally ground in a metate, producing a caramel-flavored flour that could be used as a soup, consumed as a beverage or baked into a variety of cakes.

Desert Harvest

Mesquite seeds are rich in calcium, magnesium, potassium, iron and zinc. They are about 40% protein and are high in lysine, a crucial amino acid. The bark was pounded and made into a rough fabric. Gum exuding from a wound in the tree was used to seal and mend pottery. The tree sap served as a treatment for sore throat and, when boiled, it would reduce to a black liquid paint or dye.

Ironwood and palo verde seeds were used in the same manner although they are not considered to be as versatile as the mesquite. The jojoba (ho-**ho**-ba) plant thrives in this area above 1700 feet elevation. Its seeds provided another rich source of fat and protein. All of these seeds were savored during the lengthy summer season. The surplus was roasted, parched or air dried and stored in baskets or pottery vessels.

Amaranth, sometimes known as pigweed or dragon's tongue, is a native plant that was valued both for its seeds and leaves, each high in minerals and amino acids.

The cactus family was a prolific food source, both because of the huge variety of plants and the ingenuity of the people in turning these plants to their use. It is believed that cactus has been used as a diet staple for at least 9,000 years. Researchers at the University of Arizona believe that prickly pear pads can lower blood cholesterol. Some doctors believe that the pads can also control glucose levels, avoiding the need for diabetics to use insulin.

Fiber for thongs and ropes was made from agave leaves and carbohydrates were obtained from the hearts. Archaeological evidence has been found showing that agave roasting pits were so widely used that it may have been the primary energy source in this area. The native people were usually careful not to cut all the agave in a given locale. They left some to propagate future plants. There is also evidence that agave was cultivated.

The buds of most cacti and prickly pear pads were prized as delicacies. Protein came from the seeds, especially the saguaro, which produces about 2,000 tiny black seeds in each bud. The juice of some cacti was fermented or distilled to provide alcoholic beverages.

Ocotillo roots were used to brew a tea and for its healing properties. Yucca roots were used as a soap. The plant now called Mormon Tea was used extensively for the brewing of a beverage that was believed to have both stimulative and medicinal value. Even the creosote bush, perhaps the most distasteful plant in the desert, was widely used to treat a variety of illnesses.

The native plant called "chia" produces two seed crops a year and, when mixed with water, forms a gel that has been shown to reduce cholesterol in today's population. Some doctors also believe that the type of sugars and carbohydrates in mesquite pods and seeds provide the same effect.

Native American dependence on fibrous carbohydrates through the centuries is almost surely the reason for a health problem among this population today. These desert foodstuffs were slow to be digested and the proportion of fiber to energy was large. As a result, descendants of these people are physiologically less able to tolerate some of today's foodstuffs. Modern diets include refined sugars that become quickly available in the bloodstream, thus Native Americans are more likely to become lactose-resistant, a trait that can lead to diabetes. Native people of the South Sea Islands, Australia and Southeast Asia share this same tendency.

Our desert, viewed by some as a threatening, hostile place, nourished many near its springs and river valleys. For these resourceful people, although their food supply wasn't as convenient as our local supermarket, the desert harvest was life-sustaining, often bountiful....and much less expensive!

CARLOS MONTEZUMA, M.D.
Friend Of The Yavapai

About 1865, an Indian boy named Wassaja (Wassa-jah) was born in the vicinity of today's Roosevelt Dam. His parents were members of the Yavapai tribe. Although Wassaja lived full-time among Indians for only his first six years, he was to become a national figure as a champion of Indian rights and play an important role in the ultimate destiny of his tribe. He appears often in Yavapai history and most completely in Peter Iverson's well-documented book *Carlos Montezuma*.

In 1871, during one of the many clashes between the Pima and Yavapai tribes, Wassaja and his two sisters were captured. The children were soon separated and he would never see them or his parents again. Wassaja was taken by the Pimas to a village near Florence, Arizona where they found a man of Italian descent, Carlos Gentile, who purchased the boy for $30. He was re-named Carlos Montezuma and baptized in the Church of the Assumption in Florence on Nov. 17, 1871.

Gentile moved often, giving young Carlos exposure to a variety of circumstances: first in Chicago schools, then in a one-room school near Galesburg, Ill. and later in Brooklyn, New York. When Gentile could no longer afford to support the boy, he was cared for by a Mrs. Baldwin in New York and later brought to Urbana, Ill. where a Baptist minister, William Steadman, became his guardian and later performed his wedding ceremony.

Dr. Montezuma and his wife, Marie

Grave site at the Ft. Mc Dowell cemetery

Carlos was a good student and earned grades that qualified him for a degree in chemistry at the University of Illinois in 1883. He entered Chicago Medical College, a branch of Northwestern University, and worked at a variety of part-time jobs while earning his M.D. degree in 1889.

He entered private practice in Chicago but failed to attract enough patients to earn a good living. Four assignments to Indian agencies followed---Ft. Stevenson, Dakota Territory; Shoshone Agency in Nevada; the Colville Agency in the state of Washington, and the Carlisle School in Carlisle, Pa.

At all of these locations he was critical of the Office of Indian Affairs management and the lack of opportunities it was providing, although at Carlisle he thrived and became acquainted with many people involved in national Indian policy. While there, Dr. Montezuma traveled to Arizona with the Carlisle football team in 1900. At this time he visited some of his boyhood locations and reinforced his emotional commitments to this area. He spent time with both the Yavapai and Pima people. After 2 1/2 years at Carlisle, he returned to Chicago to private medical practice.

When the McDowell Reservation was established in 1903, Carlos was corresponding regularly with several Yavapai friends and rejoiced in their return to a homeland of their choice. Dr. Montezuma also began to see that his training and experience in the white community could be used to help his native tribe.

Almost as soon as the Yavapai were located at McDowell, efforts began to move them south a few miles and attach them to the Salt River/Pima Reservation. The justification for this took many forms, one of them being the continued cost of building diversion dams in the Verde River at the head of the irrigation ditches serving McDowell. Other reasons involved water rights and the legalities that ebbed and flowed around this issue. Many groups coveted the fertile bottom land of the Verde.

Through all these many attempts to again re-locate the Yavapai, Dr. Montezuma was steadfast in his efforts to prevent it. In doing so, he earned a reputation among Indian Service people as a troublemaker. He counseled tribal elders on strategy and testified eloquently in their behalf before Congress in 1911. The same year he married Marie Keller, a woman of Romanian/American descent.

During these years Dr. Montezuma became nationally known as an advocate for better Indian education and in promoting his belief that Native Americans should be encouraged to fully participate in the mainstream of American culture. He concentrated his attention on the Yavapai, the Pima and Maricopa tribes and was outspoken in his opinion that the Office of Indian Affairs should be abolished. To that end he began a monthly newsletter in April 1916 that addressed these issues. It was appropriately named *Wassaja*. Each copy cost 5 cents and a year's subscription was 50 cents. This effort was continued on an almost-monthly basis until November of 1922. Although there were never more than a few thousand copies of each issue distributed, it clearly influenced national policy.

During the summer of 1922, the doctor developed tuberculosis. He knew that he could not continue seeing patients. In a move that tells us of his deepest feelings, he took a train to Phoenix and returned to McDowell to spend his last days. He lived there near the Dickens family in a brush shelter, living as his ancestors had for centuries. He died Jan. 31, 1923 with his wife and Yavapai friends at his side and was buried in the McDowell cemetery.

In many ways, developments since his death have vindicated his position. Just a year later, all Indians were made American citizens. Most of the changes in Bureau of Indian Affairs actions and in legislation passed have been in the direction recommended by Dr. Montezuma. He surely can be considered a "giant" in the Indian history of this valley and the entire nation.

Beeline Monument

The Ft. McDowell tribe named their new clinic the Dr. Carlos Montezuma Memorial Health Center. He is further remembered with a monument (shown above) on the south side of Beeline Highway, 1.6 miles northeast of the Shea intersection.

GENERAL IRVIN McDOWELL

We speak frequently of our Native American neighbors at the Ft. McDowell Reservation and we have often heard of the military role played by the fort in the late 1800's. In spite of the familiarity most of us have with the name, McDowell, we don't know much about the man for whom the post was named.

Irvin McDowell was born near Columbus, Ohio, Oct. 15, 1818. He was sent to a military school in France, then returned to enter West Point, graduating in 1838.

His first service was on the Canadian/New England frontier where there were border disturbances at the time. In 1841 he returned to West Point where he was Instructor of Tactics until 1845. During active duty in the Mexican War, he displayed bravery at the battle of Buena Vista, earning himself an immediate promotion to captain and soon after to major.

Mc Dowell during the Civil War

At the outbreak of the Civil War, McDowell was 43 years old and reported to be a man of great physical strength, full of energy and highly esteemed by the Union General-in-Chief, Winfield Scott. He was appointed brigadier general on May 14, 1861 and was given command of the Army of Northeast Virginia. For a few months his headquarters were in Robert E. Lee's home at Arlington, Virginia. Lee had just abandoned his family home to cast his lot with the South.

McDowell's soldiers were raw recruits and in just two months the army was thrown into the first crucial test of the Civil War, the battle of Bull Run. His Confederate opponent in the battle was Gen. P. G. Beauregard, his classmate at West Point and 2nd in the graduating class rank. McDowell was 23rd.

The Union Army was badly defeated at Bull Run. Initially most of the blame for the loss was attributed to McDowell. Historians and impartial investigators later concluded that much of the responsibility for the setback was due to actions of others outside his command. Promised reinforcements never arrived and the battlefield was crowded by visitors, official and unofficial, arriving in their carriages from Washington and other nearby towns. Bruce Catton, a noted Civil War historian, found that they observed no military restraint and "....pressed among the troops as they pleased, giving the scene the appearance of a monster military picnic." Nevertheless, McDowell became the scapegoat for the loss in the eyes of many.

General McClellan was then placed in command of the Army with McDowell assigned a division reporting to him. In April 1862, he was removed from this position and put in charge of the Army of the Rappahannock, as the primary defense of Washington D.C.

During this time McDowell reported to Army General John Pope who characterized McDowell as "....a good man and capable general but born to bad luck. The aura of failure, born of that first fight at Bull Run, trailed after him." Bruce Catton reports that "many of his troops disliked him violently, making fun of a special hat which he had devised for his summer comfort, a cool, but rather weird looking contrivance of bamboo and cloth."

McDowell was a man of iron will, consuming no coffee, tea, tobacco or alcoholic beverages. During a training exercise his horse fell on him, knocking him unconscious. When a medical officer tried to pour brandy down his throat to revive him, he was proud of the fact that he managed to keep his mouth tightly closed to prevent this "abhorrent" treatment.

At one point during General McClellan's delaying tactics and his subsequent illness in 1862, President Abraham Lincoln called McDowell and another general to Washington to counsel on strategy. Lincoln remarked at the time that "....he had to talk to somebody and if McClellan did not intend to use the Army he would like to borrow it for a time."

Under Gen. Pope, McDowell was in charge of one of three Army units at the second battle of Bull Run in 1862, which again resulted in a defeat for his troops. He was soon relieved of his command. Catton says of him "....a man unlucky beyond all other generals, taking his demotion in manful silence, without recrimination."

He was then appointed president of a court for investigating cotton frauds and for retiring disabled officers. This was considered a demotion since it was administrative in nature and not a line command.

On July 1, 1864, McDowell was placed in command of the Army's Western Division. On March 1, 1865, General John S. Mason, the commander of the Army's District of Arizona requested that McDowell send troops from California to establish a post on the Verde River. General Order #5, signed by Gen. Mason on June 15, 1865 said, "....the post will be known as Ft. McDowell."

The post's namesake visited here on Feb. 6, 1866, during an inspection trip of all camps in Arizona. He was dismayed at the poor health of the troops due to a diet deficient in fresh fruits and vegetables. He ordered all available troops to work on clearing land and re-working the Hohokam irrigation canals to establish vegetable gardens.

In 1868, he left California to be assigned to the Army's Dept. of the East. In Nov. 1872, he was promoted to major general. General U.S. Grant, then President of the United States, said at the time, "I take great pleasure in elevating McDowell to atone for what I feel were unjust charges made against him over the Bull Run losses."

July 1, 1876, he returned to the Presidio at San Francisco where he commanded the Division of the Pacific. During this time he settled many difficulties between white settlers, hunters, trappers, miners and Indians from Alaska to Arizona. He was described as squarely and powerfully built. He was said to be earnest and serious, never seeking popularity and without political aims. He was known for his fierce, unswerving patriotism.

He was placed on retired leave Oct. 15, 1882 at age 64. In retirement the California Governor, General George Stoneman, named McDowell a Park Commissioner for San Francisco ".... in view of his great practical experience in the construction of reservoirs and his general knowledge of civil engineering."

Major General McDowell died at San Francisco May 4, 1885 and is buried in the Soldiers National Cemetery at the Presidio there.

The prominence of Ft. McDowell in early Arizona history prompted the use of his name for the McDowell Mountains and McDowell Road, one of the major east-west roads in the area. From those, dozens of other commercial and public entities now use the name. Often heroic, but with two Bull Run blemishes on his otherwise distinguished career, McDowell's impact on our area is still evident.

OLD McDOWELL HAD A FARM

When Ft. McDowell soldiers first arrived in September 1865, it was a primitive outpost. The nearest dependable supply point was San Francisco. Canned goods and dried or salted meats were the standard rations.

The Last Bugle Call, by Bill Reed, and *Commanders and Chiefs*, by Fountain Hills author Elaine Waterstrat, provided the inspiration for this story of military fumblings 130 years ago.

In Feb. 1866, Gen. McDowell, for whom the fort was named, visited and was shocked by the soldier's poor health. The need for fresh fruits and vegetables was desperate, as the hospital was crowded with up to 40 cases of scurvy per day.

McDowell stopped all construction on the fort, leaving the enlisted men's barracks without roofs, putting them to work cleaning the prehistoric Hohokam canals. Others were to clear land on the west bank of the river.

His order read, in part:

> "In view of the great cost of transporting stores...of the fine land, free from alkali, in the Valley of the Rio Verde...of the quantity of water that can be made available for irrigation...of the unsettled condition of the country, on account of Indian hostilities, which has kept settlers from opening farms so far removed from the settled parts of the country, Lt. Col. Bennett will take immediate steps to open a government farm on the land. He will be authorized to hire from the discharged volunteers, 3 men at a monthly rate of 50 dollars, and 20 men at a rate of 40 dollars, and one ration each per day. He will select the most favorable place for a crib-work dam in the channel of the Rio Verde to raise the water a few feet and, from the west side of the dam, he will construct a ditch to convey water over the farm."

Actually, few discharged men were available. Most of the work was done by the cavalrymen and they suffered as a result. They were roused at 3 a.m., had to groom and feed their horses, eat a meager breakfast and walk to the site to begin at 6. Lunch was sparse and the work continued until 6 p.m. through the spring and summer. The men perspired all day, went to bed in damp clothing and chilled in the night air since the barracks were still not roofed. Severe dysentery afflicted many and several deaths occurred. After much protest, a few civilians were hired in July to help finish the work.

By Aug. 1866 the canal was restored and 240 acres of land had been cleared of brush and trees. During this time much criticism was directed at the project. The Az. Territorial Gov.,

Richard McCormick, after noting the use of soldiers for the canal, said, "For the relentless Apache, utter subjugation is admitted as a necessity. It is the primary work to which the soldier's attention must be given." The Prescott *Arizona Miner* praised Bennett for his efforts to become more self-sufficient but ended by saying, "He should be aware that the main purpose of the post is to destroy our murderous foe."

In the fall of 1866, corn and sorghum were planted but only small amounts were harvested. Ironically the crops grown on the farm were to satisfy the need for grain and forage for the horses, not to grow vegetables to improve human nutrition.

Brig. General Rusling, an Inspector General from San Francisco, visited here in July 1867. His scathing report, found in the Arizona Historical Foundation files, is excerpted here to convey its intent and his picturesque sentence construction.

> "This year's wheat crop is indifferent, having been sown too thin and irregularly. I rode over this so-called farm. It must have cost a deal of labor. I inspected their books and found them unsatisfactory. Capt. Carr and the other officers thought the farm a waste of money and a delusion. I called on Carr for a full report of the operations, to be sent to me. I received only a paper and an evasive paragraph guardedly different from what he told me at McDowell. The accounts fix nothing precisely and explain nothing. The Quartermasters Dept. may whistle when it gets anything out of this farm.
>
> By all accounts, the corn produced was immature and became rotten. If received from an outside contractor, it would have been rejected. However, this corn was fed to our animals and their bad condition when I was there was attributed partly to this.

These are financial considerations only and demonstrate the futility of this post farm. In other aspects, the farm seems to me to be defeating the objective of establishing military posts, namely to encourage and protect settlements. If we had no farm at McDowell, and the reservation was of reasonable size, settlers would occupy the valley of the Verde, and soon supply the post with all the grain needed at reasonable prices. In the end they would, of course, do away with the necessity for a post there altogether.

Now, there is scarcely a rancher there, and there will be none if the post can furnish no market for grain. So, I think, troops are enlisted and paid to scout and fight Indians--not to dig ditches and farm. Something energetic against the Apaches is expected and that this is not done, is generally charged against 'Bennett's Farm.' I am persuaded from our sorry experience that this policy is a losing one, as well as prejudicial to the morale of our soldiery.

I recommend that all farming at McDowell be prohibited hereafter, and that the reservation there be reduced to one mile square and that the valley of the Verde be thrown open to pre-emption or sale."

As we know now, the size of the post was not reduced but the farm was closed as a military project and in April of 1868 bids were taken to lease the land to private citizens. The first lessee was William Hancock, who was also the surveyor for the first Phoenix townsite in 1870 and constructed the first business building there.

Gen. Rusling was perceptive. Fort McDowell did provide a market for hay and grain and was one of the principal reasons Jack Swilling decided to clear Hohokam canals along the Salt River in late 1867 to grow these products for sale to Ft. McDowell. This was the beginning of the small village of Phoenix.

STONEMAN MILITARY ROAD
By-Passing Phoenix

Just three miles north of Fountain Hills is a former transportation artery that was the scene of great activity 128 years ago. The building of this military road was the result of an order by General George S. Stoneman.

Stoneman was born in Chatauqua County, New York on August 8, 1822. He learned surveying at the age of 17 with the intention of going to the open country of the Western United States. He was a cadet at West Point during 1842 to 1846 at which time he was a roommate of Thomas J. Jackson, later to become famous as "Stonewall Jackson."

Upon graduation with honors from West Point, Stoneman was assigned to Ft. Leavenworth, Kansas. The young lieutenant was placed in charge of an ammunition wagon train to Santa Fe where he joined the now-famous Mormon Battalion as quartermaster. This was a group of about 450 soldiers, commanded by Col. Philip St. George Cooke. They had departed Ft. Leavenworth on Oct. 1, 1846 and marched to San Diego, arriving there in February 1847. As they were crossing Arizona they were scouting for a wagon route that could serve as a trail for future travelers.

Stoneman's first singular event occurred along the Mexican border near what is now Bisbee. As the wagon train was bushwhacking through the wilderness, they encountered a herd of wild bulls on Dec. 11. During the ensuing melee two men were trampled by the bulls, one other tossed in the air, two mules were killed and Lt. Stoneman nearly shot off his thumb as his pistol accidentally discharged. No heroics yet by our young hopeful!

When the group arrived at the Gila River they were exhausted from hacking their way through the dense vegetation and rocky terrain that seemed to be associated with each waterway they were forced to follow. Col. Cooke decided to lash two wagons together, caulk them with pine tar, load them with some of the heavy provisions and float the makeshift raft down the Gila. Twenty five hundred pounds of flour, corn, some tools and portions of Col. Cooke's personal effects were destined to become the cargo. Some in the party felt this was a foolish plan but Lt. Stoneman, claiming previous boating experience, volunteered to "captain" what may have the first attempt by a white man to navigate Arizona's waterways.

The attempt was in trouble from the start. The crude vessel kept grounding on sand bars and by the end of the first day, Cooke sent a messenger to Stoneman to salvage the cargo and abandon the attempt. This message was not received, however, and the land party kept getting farther ahead. After 5 days and progress of only 54 miles Lt. Stoneman finally gave up, caching some of the supplies and discarding others that had become badly water damaged. He did float the empty platform the rest of the 20 or so miles to the Colorado Crossing near present-day Yuma. Lt. Stoneman's career doesn't appear very promising at this point!

In spite of these ill-fated events in Stoneman's first military expedition, Col. Cooke, upon arrival at San Diego, said, "I am indebted to Lts. Smith and Stoneman ...for valuable assistance, particularly in directing the pioneers (Mormons)."

Stoneman was stationed at the Presidio in San Francisco from 1848-1852 and took part in campaigns against Indians in California, Oregon and Arizona. In 1853 he escorted a survey party from California to San Antonio.

The following year he assisted Lt. John G. Parke of the U.S. Topographical Engineers in scouting out a route along the 32nd Parallel in southern Arizona. They settled on a trail just north of the Chiricahua Mountains which then became the Butterfield Overland Mail and Stagecoach route. Thus, by age 32 he had crossed Arizona three times. He was promoted to first lieutenant in 1854 and captain in 1855.

Stoneman's next notable action was at Ft. Brown, Texas at the outbreak of the Civil War where he gained fame by successfully refusing to surrender to Confederate troops. An appointment to brigadier general of the Army of the Potomac came on Aug 14, 1861 and later to major general. He was among the most noted of the cavalry leaders in the Union Army.

Gen. Stoneman during the Civil War

After the war, he was returned to his regular army rank of colonel and in August 1869 was appointed to be the first military commander of the Arizona Territory by Pres. U. S. Grant. His headquarters were at Ft. Whipple near Prescott. While here he was active, leaving his name on other landmarks such as Stoneman Lake near Flagstaff and the Stoneman Grade, a five mile wagon road west of Globe intended to connect with the infantry camp on the top of Picket Post Butte.

In July of 1870, Arizona Governor Safford invited Stoneman to attend a meeting of leading citizens of Prescott and government officials. At that session Stoneman pledged to rid the state of the Indian threat.

In late August of 1870, Col. Stoneman took an extended tour of the major Arizona Army posts and by late September he reached Ft. Mc Dowell. When the post was established in 1865, its link to civilization was by a wagon road following the approximate route of the present Beeline highway southwest from Fountain Hills. This connected McDowell to the Salt River Valley where Phoenix would later be established and on to either California or Ft. Whipple. As the Army's presence grew in Arizona, there was a need for frequent travel between posts. Ft. Whipple, near Prescott, served as the Army's headquarters but to go from Whipple to McDowell required travel through Phoenix, then back northeast.

In the late 1860's, scouting parties of cavalrymen from McDowell followed ancient Indian trails that led from the Tonto Basin, the Mazatzals and the Superstition area, then northwest from the Verde in the Needle Rock area about 14 miles north of Fountain Hills. The soldiers found that the trails converged on excellent springs in the Cave Creek area.

When Colonel Stoneman visited McDowell, he was advised of these trails and troops here urged him to expand this more direct route so that it could accommodate wagons. Stoneman said he would scout the trail himself. Most of his party took the regular road back through Phoenix and Wickenburg to Whipple but Stoneman and a small escort party took 2 ambulances (light wagons) and departed at 4 p.m. on Oct. 1, 1870. The first night they camped near what is now the intersection of Rio Verde Drive and 136th Street. The next day they managed to get to the Cave Creek springs and Stoneman decided that with concentrated effort the trail could be made passable for heavier wagons.

Soon both Whipple and McDowell troops were building the road that passed through the present McDowell Mountain Regional Park. This shortcut saved about 18 miles and also gave travelers access to abundant water. This road was used regularly from 1870 to the date of McDowell's closing in 1890. It angled northwest from the fort, crossing today's McDowell Mountain Road about one-half mile south of the entrance to the Regional Park. Maps of the park indicate the road's location and some of the hiking trails intersect with it. In most places the trail was in the sandy bottom of a major wash. In other areas erosion and vegetation have obliterated the traces.

The road passed through this wash in McDowell Mountain Park

In Cave Creek one last, clearly marked, vestige of the road remains. A street named Military Road skirts the northern flank of Black Mountain just to the south and parallel to Cave Creek Road. Early residents there say this was a part of the original road. Until very recently, it was still a gravel street.

In spite of his promises at the Prescott meeting in 1870, Stoneman did not pursue the Indians as many would have preferred. Though a decorated officer, this general was no "personality kid" ---he was variously described as abrasive, tactless and aloof. However, he treated both his friends and enemies evenly, and thus aroused the wrath of whites in Arizona when he furnished seed and farming tools, as promised, to the Apaches who came into the reservations. Until then, the pledges made to entice surrender were generally not kept. Stoneman was quoted as saying that, "The raising of crops here would consume more of the Indian's time and ingenuity than the raising of white scalps."

Territorial Governor Safford finally traveled to Washington in 1871 and was able to persuade President Grant to remove him and send General Crook to Arizona.

Stoneman retired from the Army August 16, 1871 and moved to California. He settled on a ranch in the San Gabriel Valley. In 1872, he was appointed Railroad Commissioner of California and was elected to that office at the next general election.

In 1882, he was nominated by the Democratic Party as their nominee for governor of the state. The *Tombstone Weekly Epitaph* said on June 24, 1882, "The nomination of General Stoneman by the Democrats of California is a sure guarantee of a victory at the state election. His Army record is second to none. In him was combined the dash of Custer, the skill of Jeb Stuart and the perseverance of Gen. Sheridan." He was elected Governor and served from January 1882 to January 1887.

Stoneman died in Buffalo, New York on September 5, 1894 at 72 years of age. He can be remembered as a famous military person who left his mark on our area--and our state.

DREAMS SHATTERED ON THE VERDE

A series of letters and affidavits dating from 1877 to 1906 tell a haunting tale of intrigue and conflict swirling in and around Ft. McDowell.

The story begins with the 1834 birth of Patrick White in Ireland. He immigrated to the U.S., joined the Union Army in 1855 and married Annie Dowling in June 1863.

Patrick was captured in Texas during the Civil War and became a prisoner for 22 months in Libby Prison at Richmond, Virginia. He, and others, finally escaped by using their hands and improvised tools to dig a tunnel under the fence.

White stayed in the Army and became an expert wheelwright--a wagonmaker and repairman. Annie worked as post hospital matron at a salary of $20 per month at Army posts in Wyoming and California. She also did laundry and ironing for officers and their families. They were assigned to Ft. McDowell in 1874, at which time they had four children.

In 1875, the Whites began building up a dairy herd, paying $100 each for "milch cows." They supplied provisions to the fort, receiving 10 cents a quart for milk, 50 cents a pound for butter and 50 cents a dozen for eggs.

When Patrick was discharged in 1876, after more than 21 years of service, they rented a house two miles east of the post and continued to furnish produce to the soldiers. Later that year, they bought from a Mr. Reavis the water rights to 160 acres of land on the west bank of the Verde River. In August 1877, Patrick was hired to continue his duties at McDowell, only now as a civilian, at a salary of $125 per month.

At the time they acquired the 160 acres of land, there was a question whether it was inside the military reservation. In Feb. 1877, Annie White wrote Capt. Corliss, then commander of the post, requesting permission to build a house and place 60 head of cattle on the property. Capt. Corliss replied that he had no control over the land since it was outside the reservation.

At a cost of $200 they surveyed to determine if their land could be irrigated from the Verde. They planned to bring water into a canal heading just below Needle Rock and bring it 3 miles downstream along the west bank to intersect with a portion of the ancient canals cut into the river's sandstone bank by the Hohokam.

In 1877, they heard of the Desert Land Act which allowed them to claim 640 acres of land. They exercised this claim publically on a section of land just north of their 160 acres. They also posted notices on trees at the site claiming rights to 1,000 miner's inches of water. As subsequent events were to prove, they apparently did not file the appropriate claims with the land office in Florence.

The Whites were enthusiastic about their future. Patrick had a stable income from his civilian duties at the fort and they knew there was a good market for the crops and meat they would produce from their irrigated land.

Annie White's brother-in-law, James Carroll, came here with his family in August 1878 to help with the canals. When he arrived in San Francisco, he telegraphed Ft. McDowell to tell the Whites that he would take the train to Yuma but asked how he should proceed from there. Annie later wrote that she talked to Capt. Summerhayes and that he arranged for Carroll to walk here from Yuma with a new group of Army recruits. This officer was the husband of Martha Summerhayes, who wrote the widely-acclaimed book *Vanished Arizona*.

Seven men worked nearly full time for a year on the irrigation project. This ditch was about five feet deep but varied to accommodate the needed gravity flow. Lumber was used for construction of flumes to bridge the washes coming into the Verde from the west.

In 1878, the Whites built a small house one-half mile north of the fort's north boundary. It had large rocks for the foundation, with adobe walls, a roof of mesquite limbs and saguaro ribs overlain with brush and straw and roughly plastered with mud-- very similar to the early structures at McDowell. Mexicans and friendly Indians helped them with the construction.

Things were going well for the Whites. Livestock numbers had grown as had the number of acres cleared for crops. The White Ditch, as it was then called, had been extended in a sweeping semi-circle southwest from the river, then back to the west and north, opening more acres to irrigation.

By early 1879, more than 100 acres of land had been cleared and planted. There were 60 acres of corn, 40 acres of barley and some potatoes and cabbage. These crops were harvested in November. By now over 200 acres had been cleared and they were planted to wheat and barley.

Life on the frontier was hard, but satisfying. The Whites were making plans for obtaining clear title to the land and expanding their sales of livestock and crops beyond Ft. McDowell. But trouble was approaching.

In 1879, White was fired from his McDowell job by the post commander, Capt. Chaffee, on a charge of drunkenness--a completely false claim according to the Whites and confirmed by a number of affidavits later filed on their behalf. His former commanding officer wrote about him: "I knew Patrick White as an intelligent man beyond the ordinary soldier and always a perfect gentleman."

The Whites apparently maintained good relations with other post officers for they sold 52 tons of hay and some wheat and barley to Mc Dowell during the early part of 1880.

In July 1880, Capt. Chaffee charged that the White's hogs had damaged a neighbor's irrigation ditch. A McDowell officer, Lt. Kendall, placed a stake by the side of the White's ditch one-half mile north of their house. (This stake was placed about one mile north of the present reservation line.) On July 20, Chaffee wrote the Whites to tell them they were on Ft. McDowell property and that the stake placed was the north boundary of the military reservation. He gave them 30 days to move.

Just 11 days later a detail of 12 soldiers and Lt. Kendall visited their house, removed their 7 children and household goods, put them in the desert near the present Rio Verde Ranch site, and **burned the house**. The children were helpless until other soldiers, hearing of their plight, took blankets and food to them.

When the home was burned, Annie was on her way to Prescott to challenge the notice they had received and to ask for intervention by the Territorial Governor. Patrick was upstream working on their canal.

The Whites had expected to obtain a homestead grant for the 160 acres where they had purchased water rights and a desert land title to 640 acres directly north. They also expected to solidify their claim to the Verde water. The family had 6 horses, 3 donkeys, 65 hogs, 300 chickens and 280 cattle. Their livestock scattered at the time their home was burned. The Apaches and McDowell soldiers helped themselves to the abandoned animals. All were lost. A month later the White's brother-in-law, Mr. Carroll, and his family were thrown out of their house and it was also burned. Annie later wrote, "Patrick was crazed from this event. He never again was in his right mind."

Shortly after this the Whites, now penniless and living in Tempe, applied to the War Dept. for compensation for their loss but were again told they were on military property. In 1881 and again in 1883 Capt. Chaffee accused White of selling whiskey to the Indians, but in each case he was cleared, once by a jury and the second time by a judge without trial.

Dreams Shattered on the Verde

At this same time he accused Annie White of having operated a house of ill-repute at their ranch site---a claim that was vigorously denied and affidavits supporting the Whites were signed by reputable citizens employed at the fort. In retrospect, the claim seems ludicrous since at the time there were 7 children in the White household, ages 5 months to 14, and the home in which they were living was about 12 by 20 feet with a lean-to shed on one side.

Arizona Territorial Governor Zulick asked Col. Bevens to travel from Phoenix to McDowell to investigate the incident. Bevens reported to Zulick that he found the ruins of the houses to be clearly off the reservation and that "....I consider it to be a cowardly and outrageous act."

When the post was abandoned by the military and later designated as an Indian reservation, an appropriation of $50,000 was made by Congress to buy out the claims of persons who had settled or "squatted" on their land. Investigator Frank Read ruled that the White's house and land was not on the reservation, therefore was not entitled to be settled from the $50,000. Thus, each branch of government refused responsibility---for opposite reasons.

In 1914, Annie White, in a sworn statement, listed their monetary losses as $23,375. The House of Representatives considered restitution in House Bill 257, introduced by Ariz. Rep. Carl Hayden, but it was not granted.

At this time, Annie stated that "....while they were in good financial circumstances at the time of the loss of their property for which she seeks compensation, she is now, in her old age, without means, and dependent upon others for support." Later a claim of $22,000 was introduced in Senate Bill No.1205, 60th Congress, but without sufficient backing, this did not come to a vote.

Annie White became known around Washington as "The Woman With the Black Bag" as she tirelessly pressed her case during the early years of this century. In spite of her efforts Annie was never able to get anyone to admit responsibility for the behavior of the soldiers on that fateful day in 1880.

Who was to blame? The file shows some evidence that Lt. Kendall wanted White out of his civilian job at the post so that he could appoint his own man. The Army may have had other reasons for some of their actions, though none was offered—surely no excuse can be imagined for the violent acts of arson and property destruction they caused.

Only a slight depression, small pieces of metal and large foundation stones remain at the site of the White's house

This is a remaining portion of an ancient Hohokam canal carved into the Verde bank and likely also used by the Whites

The White homesite is located just a few yards west of the west bank of the Verde and about one-half mile north of the reservation fence. Only traces of the Carroll house remain farther from the river and just north of the reservation boundary.

As a closing of the loop, the White's great-grandson, John Micek and his wife, Nancy, of Massachusetts visited Arizona to research this part of the family history. They were directed to this author who knew of the house ruins. Together, we visited the site and subsequently they have provided the documentation for this poignant story combining hopes and sorrow on the banks of the Verde four generations ago.

THE TWO FACES OF CAPT. CHAFFEE

The drama and excitement 120 years ago in the Verde valley wasn't only about Indian wars. The previous chapter told of an apparent injustice committed by Capt. Chaffee while he was commander of Ft. McDowell in the late 1870's.

The military record of Adna Romanza Chaffee tells a completely different story. Which one is correct? We may never know. Research into both sides of this bizarre series of events is instructive for it shows how one's perception of a person can be changed, depending on the reporting source.

Born in April 1842, Adna was one of twelve children of Mr. and Mrs. Truman Chaffee of Orwell, Ohio. His mother was a school teacher and his father a farmer. He was an original member of the 6th Ohio Cavalry and served with that unit for 25 years. Early in his career he was promoted to sergeant, then to lieutenant for his actions during Stoneman's Raid (the same man responsible for the Stoneman Military Road here). He saw action in 54 Civil War battles, including the Peninsula Campaign, Antietam, Fredericksburg and Gettysburg. He was wounded three times and cited for bravery twice.

Chaffee as a major in 1888

Chaffee Park in Orwell, Ohio

After the war ended, he was posted to Austin, Texas where he was quartermaster of the camp there. He decided to leave the service to enter business for himself and resigned his commission. His superiors, even Sec. of War Stanton and Gen. U. S. Grant, intervened to persuade him to remain. He did, and was again cited for bravery twice---this time for his actions in Texas during the Indian wars.

For the next 15 years he commanded troops that battled Indians in Kansas, Oklahoma, Utah, Colorado and Arizona. Although noted as a ferocious fighter, he could be compassionate. At one agency he counted 4,300 Indians imprisoned in an area equipped for 1,120 persons and insisted upon a change. He was reported as being, ".....tireless in his efforts to replace what he felt were incompetent and dishonest Indian Agents on the early reservations."

From late 1878 to 1882, he served as commander at McDowell, with a few short breaks on six occasions while he was temporarily assigned elsewhere. While here he was in charge of troops who fought in the Battle of Big Dry Wash, widely known as the last major battle with the Apaches in Arizona. This engagement took place just northeast of the present location of Strawberry. Chaffee was cited for gallantry in this encounter.

Capt. Chaffee's home at Ft. McDowell

Following his time at McDowell, he commanded Ft. Huachuca in southern Ariz. for a short time. The Chaffee Parade Field there is named in his honor. In the late 1880's, he served in New Mexico and Utah, with a promotion to major coming in mid-1888. He was appointed acting inspector general of the Army's Dept. of Arizona in the early 1890's, then to a similar position in Colorado. He was later at Ft. Leavenworth and Ft. Riley in Kansas.

Chaffee served in the Spanish-American War as a brigadier general and later became chief of staff in Havana after the war ended. He then was asked to command troops in China where they marched to the relief of Americans in Peking during the Boxer Rebellion. He served as military governor of the Phillipine Islands. His immediate predecessor there was Maj. Gen. Arthur MacArthur, father of Douglas MacArthur. During this time Pres. Theodore Roosevelt wrote him: "Believe me, my dear general, I feel very safe about the Phillipines while you command our troops there."

In 1904, Chaffee was promoted to the highest grade in the Army at that time, lieutenant general, and was appointed as chief of staff, one of only two men to achieve that status without having graduated from West Point.

He retired in 1906 after over 44 years of service. He became Chairman of the Board for the Los Angeles Public Works and was in direct control of the early construction of aqueducts by which Los Angeles could receive water from the Sierra Nevada Mountains. These actions were recently publicized in the book, *Cadillac Desert*, and the PBS series with the same name. Chaffee died in Los Angeles in Nov. 1914 and was buried in Arlington Cemetery with highest honors.

The above recitation confirms that he was a military hero and a success in his chosen career. But what kind of a man was he? What could have caused such an anomaly as the burning of the White and Carroll houses and the treatment of the White children and livestock? For insight into these questions we can only turn to what has been written about the personal side of Chaffee.

Written reports of his boyhood and military career use terms such as "disciplined," "thoroughness," "skillful," "courageous" and "full of energy" in describing him. A subordinate officer wrote: "Wherever the fire was thickest he strolled about unconcernedly, a half-smoked cigar between his teeth, and an expression of exceeding grimness on his face. Throughout the day he set the most inspiring example to his men, and that he escaped unhurt was a miracle."

Tom Horn, the subject of a chapter in this book said: "Chaffee, in a fight, can beat any man swearing I ever heard. He swears by ear, and by note in a common way, and by everything else, in a general way. An Indian would expose himself and Chaffee would swear and yell, 'Shoot, you damned idiots! What do you suppose I gave you ammunition for--to eat?' His men ....respected him."

Gen. Lawton, his commander in the Spanish-American War said of him: "I consider Gen. Chaffee one of the best practical soldiers and I shall recommend him for special distinction for successfully charging the stone fort (in Cuba), the capture of which practically ended the battle."

The *New York Herald* said when he was named chief of staff: "Chaffee is just a plain fighting man. No courtier soldier he, but a grim warrior and the bulk of whose life has been spent in hard service on the frontier...."

The Apaches spoke of him in terms of respect. They said he was...."Very severe in his notions, but a just and honest man, and harsh only with those who persisted in making, selling or drinking tizwin (the native alcoholic drink)."

The conclusion this writer makes is that Capt. Chaffee, when at McDowell, was all the things people said about him and that he was determined to impose strict discipline on all actions taken by his troops. Probably he and Patrick White disagreed violently about something--we'll never know just what it was.

Perhaps Lt. Kendall, who was subsequently accused by White of other misdeeds, decided to gain favor with Chaffee by violently carrying out the threats made in the letter to the Whites. The White family documents hint that there may have been bad feelings between the Whites and Kendall before the injustice of the home burnings.

It may be explained as a clash of wills with a violent ending that Chaffee did not envision. Clearly, he had the determination and the power to emerge the winner in this conflict on the Verde that was never reported in the effusive descriptions of his many distinguished military actions.

MARYVILLE--OUR GHOST TOWN

As we drive the Beeline Highway we're passing a bit of history that's not well known. Did you know that there was once a village near the Beeline just 4 1/2 miles southwest of Red Mountain?

We begin with the establishment of Ft. McDowell in 1865. A wagon road was built about 1868 from the fledgling settlement of Phoenix to provide supplies and mail for the camp. Ft. Whipple, near Prescott, and Wickenburg, were the population centers in central Arizona at this time. All military and commercial traffic from there to McDowell came to Phoenix and then used the new road, which followed approximately the same route as today's Beeline Highway. The Stoneman Military Road had not yet been constructed.

Persons wishing to travel to the south and east parts of the Arizona Territory from Ft. McDowell were unable to cross the Salt River anywhere east (or upstream) of the Verde-Salt confluence. The nearest suitable crossing was a shallow area about five miles southwest of Red Mountain. This became known as the McDowell Crossing and was used by Army patrols to southeast parts of the territory and by all Army traffic to and from Maricopa Wells, Yuma and California.

Maryville - Our Ghost Town

W. Earl Merrill, in a series of *Mesa Tribune* articles 30 years ago, tells that William Rowe built an adobe structure in 1868 at the point where the McDowell Crossing road joined the Phoenix-Ft. McDowell route. This became a general store catering to travelers on both roads and was operated by Charles Whitlow, who moved his family there. Troops from McDowell were among the most frequent customers. Whitlow had a 12 year old daughter named Mary Elizabeth and in her honor he named the town Maryville.

At its zenith Maryville had a general store, blacksmith shop, hotel, amateur drama troupe and several other quasi-commercial structures. Even the Tucson *Arizona Citizen*, in its July 22, 1873 edition, had a Maryville dateline that said, "Last evening we had a theatrical performance by the Maryville Amateur Troupe...It began at 8 p.m. with a reading of the Maryville *Hornet*, a paper published semi-occasionally. After the reading there was singing, recitations, comedy, etc."

The village also had a post office, which opened on April 25, 1873 and closed just eight months later. In 1870, the villages of Phoenix and Maryville were the only two valley locations shown in the census totals and their totals were combined. The numbers were: 74 dwellings and/or structures, 21 families, 192 white males, 48 white females, two black males and four black females.

Maryville existed less than 10 years. It came into being because it was the farthest upstream ford on the Salt River. During the later years, this spot was known as both the Maryville and the Whitlow Crossing. Its importance was diminished in 1870 when Charles Hayden established Hayden's Ferry on the Salt in what is now Tempe.

Indian attacks in the Red Mountain area also hastened the demise of Maryville. Several Phoenix residents on visits to McDowell were attacked in 1868 and 1869, the last being a wood hauler named Underwood. An Apache raid on Maryville May 15, 1870 caused Thomas Shortell to lose eight cows. A few days later, Thomas Rowe lost cows and oxen. Both families had small children and the loss of these dairy animals was serious. Another episode on March 29, 1874 took all of Rowe's mules and another man's only horse.

The last-known fatal encounter near Maryville took place April 14, 1874. At mid-morning Elijah Toomey and Paul Handle left Ft. McDowell with a wagon pulled by two mules. They used the Maryville Crossing and were ambushed on the south bank. Their nude, mutilated bodies were found later in the day. The wagon was intact but the two mules, which belonged to Thomas Shortell, were taken.

In 1874, Charles Whitlow wrote a letter to General Crook, sending it to the commanding officer of McDowell for forwarding, in which he requested that a military escort be posted at Maryville to accompany and protect travelers in the vicinity. There were only three men left there, himself, J.J.Wilson and Allen Whitlow. There is nothing in the record to show that this plea was answered.

Whitlow left in late 1874, moving his family to Florence, Arizona, where he owned a large ranch. His son, Charles, Jr., became a prominent citizen in the area with a dam bearing his name built to protect Williams Field from flash floods. The Charles Whitlow Rodeo Ground south of town is also named for him.

By the time the first Mormon pioneers arrived in 1877, Maryville was a ghost town. The group, which became known as the Lehi party, left Salt Lake City with 22 wagons and 84 people in January and arrived at the crossing on March 6.

Daniel W. Jones, the party's leader wrote:

"We are encamped on the banks of the Salt River, just below the junction of the Rio Verde, thirteen miles from Camp McDowell. The stream here is about 200 yards wide, and runs along with a splashing sound that seems very grateful and delicious after coming off the desert. High mountains a few miles east enclose the haunts of the Pinal and Tonto Apaches, who roam all over the country through which we have been traveling. A grand 'askia' (meaning acequia, Spanish for canal) starts from where we are and reaches out upon the desert 20 to 30 miles; large as the Erie Canal and a monument of the patient race that perished with the Montezumas."

Maryville - Our Ghost Town

The Mormons immediately began enlarging and improving the old canals, which were badly eroded at that time. The four canals fed by this supply point irrigated an estimated 140,000 acres to the south and west. With only 20 adult males doing most of the work, four miles of the canal were cleared by July 4th to the vicinity of today's Horne and Lehi Road intersection in Mesa. At this point they established Fort Utah. Cottonwood logs and timbers from the abandoned Maryville site were recycled by the pioneers to build the fort and the first houses in Lehi. At that time the nearest source of finished lumber was Prescott.

Daniel Jones later wrote:

"During the latter part of 1877, I was sent a number of times to Ft. McDowell for supplies. The distance was not great, about 20 miles, but the trip was quite dangerous. There were a number of graves in the canyon (the present Beeline route) between Lehi and the fort. My trips were made mostly on Saturdays. Often, I would have to stay late because the butcher never killed until near sundown, and I had to wait for the meat. It was always dark when I came down over the divide and down the canyon past the graves. I was always a little nervous and was glad when I arrived back home."

This is the same trail mentioned by Martha Summerhayes in her book, *Vanished Arizona*, when she writes of her Dec. 1876 arrival in the McDowell vicinity.

"As we wound our way through this deep, dark canyon, after crossing the Salt River, I remembered the things I had heard, of ambush and murder. The soldiers were not partial to McDowell canyon; they knew too much about the place; and we all breathed a sigh of relief when we emerged from this dark, uncanny road and saw the lights of the post, lying low, long, flat, around a square."

There are two unique markers on the south side of the Salt commemorating the crossing and the Lehi party. To see them, travel to the Gilbert/McDowell Road intersection. Go east one-half mile and turn left on Lehi Road. Continue on Lehi one and one-half miles---this is just eight-tenths of a mile past the Orange Patch store. Watch for the sand and gravel business on the left. Just past their entrance you'll see two brick pillars on the left, each with a wagon wheel on top. These frame a large, inscribed wooden marker.

A monument was erected at the crossing site on the south bank of the river. The marker was placed by the Mesa Boy Scout Troop 57 and says: "To all Mormon Pioneers Who Camped Here 1877." Erected in 1931 and restored in March 1982 by Aaron Beaty, it now stands near the wooden sign.

The sign on Lehi Road   *The Lehi monument*

Having walked the Maryville site three times in recent years, the author can report that there are many items of debris scattered about, but most are likely dated to the last 50 years. A few signs of Native American habitation still exist. Some are from the ranching era in the decades just before and after 1900. Others may be Maryville.

In the late 1960's, Earl Merrill took pictures of rock walls and other features that were likely the last traces of this singular, short-lived village. They were located just southwest of the present

Maryville - Our Ghost Town

Red Mountain Trap and Skeet shooting range. Based on maps found at the Arizona Historical Foundation, the village was about 1/4 mile south of the Beeline milepost 184.

Merrill also reports that an Indian cowboy showed him two stone-covered graves near the town site. The cowboy said that the Pimas called this village "Sa-a-rick," which meant "many children" and that two were buried here. This author notes that Sawik Mountain is just across the Beeline north of this spot. It would seem that this Pima word was the origin of this mountain's name. Another place-name book states that Sawik is from the Pima words, "sah" (meaning red) and "wick" (meaning mountain). Thus, we have a choice.

A visit to the markers on Lehi Road and an occasional glance toward the old town site as we drive the Beeline will remind us of the hardships, dangers and uncertainties of life in our vicinity 125 years ago.

McDOWELL/RENO MILITARY ROAD
The Trail to Conflict

Ft. McDowell was established in 1865 and immediately provided some protection for the settlers and miners who were beginning to populate this area. The Indians were at home in the rugged mountains to the east, however, and it was not unusual for them to raid white settlements for horses, food and weapons, then retreat to the hills where they were difficult to find or to engage in battle. It must be remembered that by this time the whites had displaced the Indians from their prime hunting grounds along the Gila, Salt and Verde rivers.

In the past they had spent their summers in the mountains and winters in the valleys, following the most benign weather and the harvest of the seasonal native plants. Now as they were forced to spend more time in the hills, the stress sometimes made them reckless in their struggle for existence. This pattern triggered a military decision to pursue them with the establishment of a fort in the Tonto Creek basin.

This move was based on the difficulty of long expeditions from Ft. McDowell into the wilderness area to the northeast. Packing supplies and equipment into this tortured mass of rock, catclaw, and manzanita took so much time and energy that there was little left to take on the adversary.

McDowell/Reno Military Road

In September 1867, officers William Mills, George W. Chilson and Richard Dubois were made responsible for building the new post. Mills soon became commander of Ft. McDowell and Dubois was placed in charge of opening a route to the site.

In October 1867, the road builders crossed the Verde River 1/2 mile north of Sycamore Creek with a party of 40 pack mules, one wagon and two companies of infantry.

The troops took part of their rations with them "on the hoof." These cattle and the mules attracted Apache interest and they stampeded the stock twice in the first few weeks. The Prescott *Arizona Miner* misunderstood the expedition for they said at the time, "Two companies of infantry is too small a force to be able to accomplish much in the way of killing Indians. We rather think they will be kept busy enough watching the stock and other govt. property belonging to the camp, without scouting."

The road headed northeast along the north side of Sycamore Creek. Twelve miles from Ft. McDowell they hit the Mazatzal foothills and the heavy work began. Much blasting was required and supply trains were constantly shuttling back to McDowell for food and dynamite.

On Oct. 30, they had progressed to Toddy Mountain (today's Sugarloaf Mtn.). By Nov. 11, the road extended 20 miles and Camp Miller was established on the west bank of Sycamore Creek and just west of Beeline Highway at about milepost 209. Camp Miller had a hospital tent, livestock corrals, storage facilities and an administrative office tent. By Dec. 2, another 5 miles was built and Camp Eagle became the road builder's new frontier.

On Dec. 11, Camp Carroll was built. This location was at the present Beeline highway 1/4 mile north of Sycamore Creek at milepost 213. The camp was named for 1st Lt. J.C. Carroll who had been killed by Apaches one month earlier. By the end of Jan., in spite of cold weather and flooding, the road was open to a point near where Sunflower is now located. Camp Carroll was abandoned and Camp O'Connell established here. This spot was named for Major John O'Connell, a Civil War officer who died earlier that year.

Severe weather was encountered in February 1868---only one mile of road was completed. By early April, crews were within 1/2 mile of the summit of the Mazatzal range and just 7 miles from the proposed interim destination near Tonto Creek. By May only three more miles were finished--the terrain was extremely rugged at this portion of the road. Some observers said they doubted if harder work had ever been done by soldiers in Arizona.

By the end of June, a road was completed east close to Tonto Creek. In late July, 80 men pushed on north along the west side of the creek, reaching what was expected to be the camp's permanent location in Green Valley. This was considered a choice spot but was too far from Ft. McDowell and they withdrew to the previous site. On Oct. 3, 1868, this location was designated Camp Reno, named for Major General Jesse Reno, who was killed early in the Civil War.

From the beginning, Camp Reno was staffed with only a skeleton force. A large number of soldiers were needed to guard and manage the numerous supply wagon trains that had to shuttle between there and Ft. McDowell. Supplies were expensive since it was a hard three-day trip from McDowell. Delivered costs to Reno were $59 per ton for hay and $5.75 per bushel for corn and barley.

On Feb. 17, 1870, only 16 months after the opening of Reno, Inspector General Lt. Col. George W. Wallace arrived for an inspection. His report says, in part:

> "The only road is the McDowell trail and it is exceedingly rough and rocky, the elevations and depressions of which I consider impracticable for loaded wagons....I recommend that the troops be withdrawn and the site abandoned. The expense of retaining a command here is very great. The forage for one horse amounts to $1.62 per day."

McDowell/Reno Military Road

The Reno site is fenced to prohibit motorized vehicles

A few rock foundations are all that remain

By April 1870, Camp Reno was closed and on June 2, 1870 Apaches burned the haystack and buildings. This enormous amount of effort was largely wasted except for the fact that McDowell soldiers used this road for the first leg of military patrols to the north and east for the next 20 years.

The road was subjected to various sorts of deterioration after the closing. It is well established that it was used by Mc Dowell troops in the 1870's and 80's as they scouted under Gen. Crook in the Tonto Basin wars.

The road again made history in 1892 when it was used by Ed Tewksbury, one of the principals in the final killing of the infamous Pleasant Valley War. He used this route for his seemingly impossible 170-mile round trip ride from the Young, Az. area to Mesa and back in a 24 hour period. To accomplish this feat, he used a relay of at least five horses (some sources say more). While he was in Mesa, he apparently murdered Tom Graham, the last surviving member of the Graham family. Tewksbury was identified by a Justice of the Peace as he rode hard past Sugarloaf Mountain, just northeast of Fountain Hills. But that's another story as documented many times, most recently by Don Dedera in *A Little War of Our Own*.

It wasn't much of a road--really just a glorified trail, but it provided the best route available for a lot of varied personalities 125 years ago.

It became a mail route in the late 1800's as others used it to populate the Payson and Mogollon Rim country. It also provided early access to the copper mines of Globe and Miami. When construction of Roosevelt Dam began in 1902 a road through Globe and the Apache Trail were constructed and were more easily traversed.

In modern times some portions of the original road have been used by 4-wheel drive vehicles. Other parts have been destroyed by the construction of the Bush, and later, Beeline highways which closely followed its route through the Mazatzal foothills in the vicinity of milepost 211 to 220. Some sections of the road, especially the last few miles near Reno Pass, are still vaguely defined.

In 1982 and '83, a group of archaeology students researched this route. The students were led by Julie Hoff and Jim Stute. The research was summarized by Hoff in a paper presented to the Southwest Archaeological Association in 1984 and titled *The Historical Archaeology of the Reno Road, Arizona.*

Aerial photographs from the Arizona Department of Transportation were used as a starting place but the on-site effort was a case of surveying a 20-yard-wide strip of land along the likely route by walking, then through the use of metal detectors seeking artifacts that could verify or refute the presence of the military road. It is likely that many surface items had been recovered by relic hunters in the century since the road was heavily used and the date of this survey. Most items found on this survey were buried so detectors were essential.

Artifacts recovered were mapped and dated. Throughout the entire length of the road enough objects were recovered to positively identify the route. In the few miles just east of the Verde River, the flat, open terrain had no trace of the old road except for a modern 4-wheel-drive trail which was identified by artifacts as being the Reno road.

Two ranch sites were encountered along the Reno road, one being the Adams (Romo) ranch just three miles east of the Verde and the other at Sheep Crossing on Sycamore Creek near Sugarloaf

McDowell/Reno Military Road

Mountain. No collections were made at these sites although many traces of activities dating in the early 1900's were identified.

In some places it was possible to identify the road since rocks had been pushed aside to partially smooth the trail, forming parallel rows usually about 2 feet high and 7 feet apart (the width that would allow an Army wagon to pass). Some small washes are still partially filled with rocks placed there by soldiers to even the grade.

Extant sections of the Reno Road in 1983

Artifacts were counted and grouped as follows:

```
Kitchen ----------------Cans and glass                    24%
Architecture------------Nails                             41%
Activities -------------Harness pieces, horseshoes
                        and horseshoe nails,
                        wagon parts, ammunition
                        and tools                         25%
Personal ---------------Civilian arms, clothing
                        and misc. gear                    10%
```

Patterns emerged as the location of each item was mapped and grouped by category. The highest densities were, as might be expected, near the four work camps: Miller, Eagle, Carroll, and

O'Connell. Excavations at these camps were done as a separate project by Professor Gary Shaffer and some of his students from Scottsdale Community College.

At Camp Miller there were significant quantities of Minie' balls (which became commonly known as Minnie balls). These were .58 caliber lead balls that were widely used in the Civil War. They were named for the French inventor, Captain Claude Minie'. Also found there were 2 chess pieces carved from Minnie balls, a broken straight razor and a Mexican coin.

High artifact numbers were also found near Reno Pass east of Sunflower where 3 miles of less disturbed road was found. Large clusters of Spencer repeating rifle cartridges were found just two miles east of the Verde River where a clash with Apaches apparently took place.

An Army belt buckle, bullets and old glass bottles were typical of items found. One of the bottles has the inscription "Jamaica Ginger" and "PHILAD", apparently an abbreviation for Philadelphia.

Many tin remnants were found--oil and vegetable cans, coffee cups, coffee cans and many seafood cans shaped like today's sardine cans, some with the labels still visible. These once contained crab, shrimp, lobster, sardines and fish canned in New England, shipped around the southern tip of South America to the West Coast or Gulf of California, then overland in supply wagons to these remote frontiers.

There were many kinds of glass debris--mostly purple, green and dark blue in color. There were some intact bottles, many with the manufacturers mark clearly visible. Some .70 caliber Sharpe's ammunition was found---even unfired rounds. One 12-gauge metal shotgun shell casing was found--a rarity in those days. Nearly all the rifle and carbine shell casings were smashed by the soldiers with their boot heels, a practice required in this country; otherwise the Indians would retrieve the intact casings, trade for powder and shot and then re-load their own shells.

Wagon parts were most numerous along the rougher sections, reflecting the fact that it was here where the most damage occurred to equipment. There was even a cluster of wagon debris at one rugged location, causing the archaeologists to surmise that a wagon had turned over and was partially destroyed at that point. This could also have been the site of one of the several documented skirmishes with Indians that occurred along the road.

The author has walked the sites of Camps Eagle, Carroll and O'Connell in recent years just prior to the widening of Beeline Highway. All were adjacent to the highway and on ridges near creeks. To the casual observer the locations are not unusual. But close examination shows traces of rock rings used as fire pits, evidence of cleared areas where tents were pitched or horses stabled and a rock pile probably used by the blacksmith for shoeing horses and for wagon and harness repair. Standing here causes one to make the extraordinary comparison between the activity that occurred here during the building and use of this road with the hum of Beeline traffic now.

AL SIEBER---ARIZONA'S FIRST "SCOUTMASTER"

Many famous men spent time at Ft. McDowell during its military history, but none more renowned at the time than Army scout, Al Sieber, who was here on many occasions during the 1880's. He was a master scout and the "master" of a group of Apache and Pima scouts who played a crucial role in the Indian battles then.

Sieber was born in Germany's Rhineland in 1844 but was reared in Pennsylvania. He was living in Minneapolis, Mn. when he enlisted as a Union soldier in the Civil War.

He was in the middle of the Battle of Gettysburg, being wounded twice, one bullet entering his leg at the ankle and exiting near his knee. He always limped from his wounds, but was known as a tall and well-built soldier who spoke with a strong German accent and was absolutely fearless.

Sieber participated in more battles than the combined total of Daniel Boone, Jim Bridger and Kit Carson. He shot more Indians than all three combined, yet he was as respected by the Indians as any of the army scouts in the West.

He was with General Stoneman and General Crook during the early battles in the 1870's. General Crook brought a new technique to the Indian warfare in Arizona. Crook noted that many of the tribes had a history of fighting among themselves just as fiercely as they battled the army. His strategy, which ultimately proved to be effective, was to hire Indians from friendly tribes to be his scouts. These Indian allies were better able to find hostile groups and advise the army how to subdue them.

Al Sieber - Arizona's First "Scoutmaster"

In Dec. 1873, Sieber, with 14 Tonto scouts, were in the Sycamore Creek area just east of Ft. McDowell. In bitter cold and snow they attacked an Indian camp. One of those killed was the mother of one of the scouts. It was necessary to lay over for 2 days so that the scout could fulfill the Indian's required period of mourning.

The soldiers and scouts then went west to the Cave Creek area where they successfully ambushed a large group of Indians in the caves that gave the creek its name. In 1874, the Prescott *Arizona Miner* reported after another Sieber tracking and killing that, "The west side of the Verde, between Camp Verde and McDowell, is now entirely free of hostiles."

In 1876, he and a Major Brayton were on a mission to avenge the death of a prospector who had been killed by Indians on Tonto Creek. In two quick strikes, they captured them near Fossil Creek. By this time they were low on rations and came to Ft. McDowell for supplies, including grain for their horses. They stayed 3 days, left for another battle on the west slopes of Four Peaks, then scouted both sides of the Verde River in the Needle Rock vicinity.

Sieber was the primary negotiator with Geronimo during an 1878 foray into Mexico. Sixty-two Indians did return to the San Carlos Reservation, as requested but their chief was not among them. On frequent occasions Sieber was either the lead scout in the tracking and the battles or was involved in interpreting the tense discussions with Geronimo and other Apache chiefs.

In 1882, Sieber was assigned to McDowell while Capt. Adna Chaffee was commander. While here, he wrote his account of the "Loco Campaign," a bloody trip from southeast Arizona 30 miles into Mexico in pursuit of the Chiricahuas. While on the McDowell payroll, his salary was $125 per month.

It was from here that he and his scouts took the old McDowell/Reno military road to meet Indians at what came to be known as the Battle of Big Dry Wash. This would subsequently be called the last major conflict between the Army and Apaches in Arizona. The action began when natives on the San Carlos and Ft. Apache Reservations broke out of the loosely guarded compounds. The group of about 75 warriors, were led by a chief named Nan-tia-tish, sometimes called Na-ti-o-tish.

Their first foray was against McMillanville, a small mining camp near Globe but they were turned away. From there they ranged north, killing several settlers on ranch sites between Globe and the Mogollon Rim. At the Isadore Christopher Ranch, for whom Christopher Creek was named, they burned his two log houses but he was away from his homesite and survived. They then killed others along the East Verde River.

By this time the Army was besieged by urgent pleas from the settlers for some sort of retaliation. Troops from all the forts in the area were mobilized. Al Sieber and 8 Tonto Apache scouts were among them, leaving Ft. McDowell July 6, 1882. About 350 troops would eventually be involved with 150 fully-loaded mules, all converging on the fleeing Indian's trail which now led up the Mogollon Rim directly north of Payson. As they were climbing, the Apaches could see the pursuing troops. They devised an ambush but Sieber and his clever scouts discovered it and alerted the troops in time to avoid the trap. When Chaffee's cavalry troops finally caught them it was in the Big Dry Wash canyon, now known as East Clear Creek. The intense battle occurred on July 17th. The Indians were subdued and from that date most larger bands were confined to reservations.

Obviously a posed picture of Sieber. He once said of his scouting costume, "It was ever the same as that of any roving man."

The need for Army scouts rapidly diminished although occasional expeditions would continue for several years. Sieber's fame was such that a creek in Gila County, a mountain in the Bradshaw Mountains and a Grand Canyon overlook point was named for him. By the late 1800's he had left the Army and turned to prospecting. He owned a claim in Jerome in the 1870's but abandoned it without enjoying any of the riches it later produced. At one point he opened a brewery in Bisbee with a bar in the front but that lasted only a short time.

He lived in Globe, then at Roosevelt, a village at the site of the dam. Associates described him as a crack shot, never married and with no real home. He was not outgoing and slow to accept a stranger. He rarely used profanity or consumed alcohol. When he did drink excessively he talked too much but, unlike many others, he had sense enough to know he was drunk and would roll up in his bedroll and sleep it off.

He would sometimes ride from Roosevelt to Mesa and back (60 miles) in a day. When Roosevelt Dam was being constructed, Sieber was in charge of a crew of Indians building a road to the site, today's Apache Trail, then beyond the dam along the west side of Tonto Creek.

Conflicting stories survive to tell of his untimely death at age 63. One says that the crew rolled a huge boulder onto him, killing him instantly. Dan Thrapp, in his excellent book, *Al Sieber, Chief of Scouts,* believes that he was working on the downside of the grade, trying to dislodge the rock when it suddenly fell on him. The optimist in us would like to believe the latter version and it does seem to have the most authenticity.

When the news of his death was received in Phoenix, the Arizona Territorial Legislature adopted a 210-word resolution and eulogy and adjourned for the rest of the day in honor of this tough frontier scout.

A huge crowd attended his funeral in Globe, where he is buried. Later that year he was honored by the placing of a monument carved from native stone by Apache stonecutters. It still stands today across the road from the spot of his death about 1 mile north of Roosevelt Dam. The inscription on the stone is exactly as shown here:

The inscription is shown at left

AL SIEBER
VETERAN OF THE CIVIL WAR AND FOR TWENTY YEARS A LEADER OF SCOUTS FOR THE U.S. ARMY IN ARIZONA INDIAN TROUBLES. WAS KILLED ON THIS SPOT FEBRUARY 19TH, 1907 BY A ROLLING ROCK DURING CONSTRUCTION OF THE TONTO ROAD HIS BODY IS BURIED IN THE CEMETERY AT GLOBE.

Life was exacting 125 years ago in central Arizona and Al Sieber, chief of scouts, proved that he was up to the challenge.

TOM HORN
Good Guy--or Bad?

Tom Horn has not become a familiar name to most, yet this former Ft. McDowell interpreter gained fame beyond that which he enjoyed while stationed here. His duties at McDowell involved using his language skills in speaking Spanish and Apache during the 1880's.

His autobiography, *The Life of Tom Horn*, was written in a Wyoming jail in 1903 as Tom awaited the hangman's noose for a crime he may not have committed.

Born in northwest Missouri in 1860, Tom loved the outdoors and was a "quick study." By the time he was 14 he was driving a stagecoach on the Santa Fe-Prescott route. The following year he was at Camp Verde where he met the famed scout, Al Sieber, who hired him as an interpreter at $75 per month and taught him how to follow a trail, no matter how obscure. Apache Chief Pedro, after meeting Horn, invited him to live with his tribe. Sieber encouraged this, for he felt it would make young Tom even more valuable as he learned how the Apaches lived and reasoned.

Horn was at the San Carlos Agency in 1877 where he was involved in many campaigns, even pursuing bands of Chiricahuas into Mexico, causing the Arizona Military Dept. to praise him in writing for three separate acts of bravery. His salary at this time was $100 per month. His was an intimidating presence--6 feet tall and 200 pounds--larger than the average man in those days.

In 1878, funds to continue the pursuit of Indians were cut off, so the scouts looked for other employment. This took Horn to Tombstone where he was involved with Ed Schieffelin at the time of his silver strike that made the town famous. Horn and Seiber staked a claim there and in a few weeks sold it for $2,800.

Soon the scouts were re-hired and now Horn was also serving as chief scout on some expeditions. He was known as a friendly, popular person who used no profanity, an attribute that no doubt separated him from many of his contemporaries. During this period Horn visited Ft. McDowell on several occasions and was stationed here in 1882 and 1883.

He was active in Southeast Arizona and Mexico in General Crook's campaign against Geronimo's band in 1886. After they surrendered, the Army's need for Horn was over. Tom went to the Young, Arizona area where the Pleasant Valley War was raging and, though in the middle of the controversy, apparently never became closely tied to either faction. He also served as a deputy sheriff in both Yavapai and Gila counties.

On July 4, 1888 he won a bull-dogging contest at a Globe rodeo. Each county winner came to Phoenix to the Territorial Fair to compete for the championship. A clipping from the *Philadelphia Times* states:

> "....Tom Horn won the contest, time 49 1/2 seconds, which has not since been lowered. ....Horn is well known all along the border. He served as government guide, packer, scout and as chief of Indian scouts....He is the hero referred to in the story of 'The Killing of the Captain,' by John Heard, Sr., published some months ago in the *Cosmopolitan* magazine."

Tom Horn

Tom Horn

From this time until World War I, there was a lariat rope on the market called the "Tom Horn."

For another year and a half he worked on a mining claim near Winkelman, Arizona, which he sold for $8,000 in 1890. He was with the Pinkerton Agency in Colorado, successfully tracing and arresting train robbers for two years. He then was employed by a cattle company in Wyoming where rustling had become a major problem.

While serving in this capacity, his lifetime of violence seemed to grow into a viciousness that had not previously been evident. He openly boasted of his prowess as a "hired gun." He did not deny that he killed--he even perhaps embellished his success for it served his purpose in discouraging the rustlers.

He then served in the Spanish-American War and was chief packmaster in charge of 520 mules and 133 packers for Lt. Col. Theodore Roosevelt and his Rough Riders. Through his ingenuity the mules were swam ashore safely from transport ships since landing vessels were not available. Just a few hours before the battle of San Juan Hill, Col. Leonard Wood and Roosevelt met him and received fresh animals for the famous assault.

After the war, Horn worked for the Wyoming Stock Owners Ass'n. as a detective, continuing the work he had done so well before. To enhance his reputation he would often refer to himself as the rustler's bogeyman. He would agree with others that killing was his stock in trade. "I'm an exterminatin' son of a bitch," he was quoted as saying. This bravado would later doom him in the courtroom.

Two families in the district were the Millers and the Nickells. By the turn of the century they had been feuding for a decade. In 1901, the Nickells brought sheep into the district, a serious sin in the eyes of most cattlemen. In July 1901, 14-year-old Willie Nickell was found shot to death. Two weeks later, Willie's father was also shot, the bullet breaking his arm. While he was in the hospital, a gang of masked men clubbed his sheep to death. There were no clues but most felt that one of the Millers was responsible.

However, on Jan 13, 1902, Horn was arrested and charged with the Nickell boy's murder. The most damaging evidence against him was a "confession" Horn made to a U.S. Marshall during a lengthy drinking bout. There were concealed witnesses in a room adjacent to the hotel room where the marshall got Tom bragging about his prowess as a killer of cattle rustlers and then led him into a discussion of the Nickell boy's death.

Al Sieber, when he heard that Horn was accused of murder, wrote to Cheyenne in Tom's behalf, saying: "A more faithful or a more honorable man I never met in my life. I can not, and will not, ever believe that Tom was the man the papers tried to make the world believe he was."

After a two-week trial in Cheyenne, he was found guilty in Oct. 1902. Appeals to the Wyoming Supreme Court and the Governor were unsuccessful and on Nov. 20, 1903 he was hanged in Cheyenne.

It was said that Horn was the coolest person present at his hanging. As he was led to the gallows, he looked at the group of lawmen who had gathered to witness the hanging and said to the local sheriff, "Ed, that's the sickest looking lot of damned sheriffs I ever seen." The hangman, a deputy sheriff named Higby, was a Cheyenne native but moved to Phoenix in 1948 at age 81, living at 1805 W. Weldon.

In Sept. 1993, Horn was re-tried in Cheyenne by those who have kept this celebrated and controversial case alive. The mock trial took two days and included Tom's great-great-niece as one of the defense attorneys. This time he was acquitted---just 91 years too late!

Thirteen books and dozens of articles have covered this story of an impressive figure in Southwestern history who may have been over-zealous in his pursuit of "range justice." It again reminds us of the colorful personalities that inhabited Ft. McDowell during its busy times.

BOX BAR RANCH

Just 8 miles north of Fountain Hills, one of the major ranch sites in the area once existed. It was unique in that it involved privately owned land and was located on the banks of the Verde River. Even now the spot that was the Box Bar Ranch headquarters is one of only two privately owned parcels of river frontage land between the mouth of the Verde and Camp Verde.

During the late 1800's, the Arizona rancher grazed his cattle wherever he could find good grass and water. These were bonanza years for the range was free, the competition from other cattlemen for prime sites was minimal and the Eastern demand for beef was insatiable. The only negative to this scenario was the difficulty and high cost of getting animals from the Arizona range to packing plants and to the consumer.

In 1915, just three years after Arizona became a state, W.W. Moore and Frank Asher formed the Box Bar, leasing 92,000 acres of government land. They established a brand that contained a square with a diagonal line inside. The brand (shown below) was formally registered Sept. 15, 1919.

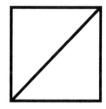

The ranch was along the Verde as far north as the present Bartlett Lake and east to the Maverick Mountain area in the Mazatzals. It extended south to the present northern boundary of the McDowell Reservation and six miles west.

One of the partners has been memorialized by the naming of two small mountains 3 miles west of the ranch site as "Asher Hills."

On June 23, 1916, Moore purchased half of Asher's share of the livestock on the ranch, giving him a 3-year mortgage for $26,000 at 8% interest. A document was found showing that on Nov. 27, 1916, Moore settled with Tonto National Forest for having 430 more cattle on his range than was permitted. He agreed to pay the standard fees that were due but successfully pleaded that he not be assessed any penalty since the range east of the river was so rough that he couldn't accurately determine the number he had.

On Sept. 27, 1919, Asher received title to 157 acres of homestead land fronting on the west bank of the Verde in a land grant signed by President Wilson. He sold his interests to Moore in 1922.

Moore was a deputy sheriff, as were many of the more respected ranchers of that era. In the mid-1920's, he tracked a bank robber east of the Verde and eventually killed him somewhere near where the road to Four Peaks branches off the Beeline highway. He tied the outlaw to the back of his saddle and delivered him into downtown Phoenix. Moore kept the robber's pistol with the initials "K.T." on it. The name, however, has not survived the test of time.

The Box Bar headquarters was considered one of the finest in the area since it was on the river and because of the special care given the site by the Moores. In the front yard there was a large cement-lined pond stocked with goldfish. From the pond an irrigation pipe led to Mrs. Moore's garden which was reported to have been "large and productive."

Mr. Moore would go to Phoenix in a wagon for provisions only about every two months. His grandson, W.W. "Buzz" Davies, recalled in 1985 that he would always include whiskey on his shopping list for his own use but the cooperative provisioners would manage to list it as something else since Mrs. Moore reviewed the bills and strongly disapproved of alcoholic beverages.

Many of W.W. Moore's earliest invoices prior to the Box Bar partnership are still in the possession of Mrs. Flora Belle Davies, of Scottsdale, widow of Buzz Davies, and are from M. Jacobs, General Merchandise, Phoenix (no street address shown). Examples of early purchases are:

Dec. 4, 1886	61 lbs. Beans	$3.05
Dec. 31, 1899	10 lbs. Peaches	1.50
	7 lbs. Bacon	.88
	1 pr. Overalls	.90
	25 lbs. Potatoes	.52
	1 lb. Tea	.50
Mar. 9, 1904	1 Washboard	.65
	3 lbs. Arbuckle coffee	.45
June 16, 1905	10 lbs. Flour	1.60

Another remarkable feature from the past can be found nearby. In a box canyon about eight miles east of the ranch are the ruins of an enclosure made of stone. This was known as "rustlers' corral" where, in the early 1900's, horse thieves would hold stolen animals to change brands and ready them for shipment to buyers throughout the state. Ruins of a stone shelter were still there in the 1930's but only traces remain now.

W.W. Moore's sons continued to operate the Box Bar after he died in 1929. In 1955, the ranch was sold to Will Ryan of Globe who sold it to Francis Curtis in 1957.

In the late 50's, the Paradise Valley Water Co. tried to get Curtis to sell them water rights, for the supply of sub-surface water is enormous at this spot. The Page Land and Cattle Co., of Phoenix, realizing this and sensing the possibility of future development in this then-isolated portion of Maricopa County, attempted to trade land they owned in northeast Arizona for the ranch but Curtis would not agree. Finally an outright purchase by Page was made in 1960.

In 1978, Jerry Robinson, a cowboy at the Box Bar, found an old Wells Fargo strong box on top of one of the mountains about two miles northeast of the ranch. The top had been broken open, it was empty and badly weathered, but still clearly marked. We'll likely never know the rest of that story!

East of the river there were numerous springs but to the west, water was scarce. Thus, the cattle generally grazed far into the mountains on the east side. The rougher country there made life extremely difficult for the cowboys. At roundup time dogs were used to drive individual cows out of canyons and to collect strays. Even so, it was usually necessary to rope and lead out many of the animals, obviously a much more time-consuming task than a roundup on the plains.

Grazing and roundup procedures have not changed a lot in the last century but the marketing process is much different. Cattle from the Box Bar used to be driven along the Verde to a point where the Ft. McDowell irrigated land is located. There they would be watered, allowed to graze and rested overnight.

The next day they would be driven to a point about four miles east of the Pavilions shopping center, where the same overnight procedure would occur. The third day they followed Indian School Road to the Lynn pasture at the corner of Hayden and Indian School. On the fourth day the herd would continue west to 19th Avenue, then south to the railroad tracks and holding pens there.

Often they could be loaded directly on rail cars but sometimes a wait of another day was incurred, adding to the loss of weight since leaving the ranch. Then a train ride of several days followed as the animals were transported to packing plants in California, Ft. Worth, Kansas City or Omaha. Today, semi-trailers load at the ranch and within 12-36 hours the cattle are at their ultimate destination.

The Box Bar Ranch is now owned by those who have developed Rio Verde and Tonto Verde. Since their purchase of the remaining ranch property and the grazing rights in 1984, they have elected to let the allotment lapse. Thus, after about 100 years of intensive use, this part of our wilderness is again returning to its natural state. The ranch property is closed to the public and used as a housing site for some employees, for water wells and a picnic area serving both communities.

In the evening, with a full moon rising over the Mazatzals and the Verde splashing away the silence, it's an inspiring scene. At these times, it is easy to imagine the night sounds of long ago when this place was a busy ranch headquarters.

P-BAR RANCH
Fountain Hills' Birthplace

Like many Arizona cities, Fountain Hills is located on land once used as an active cattle ranch. Unlike most others, the ranch headquarters was still present on the town site when development work started in the early 1970's. This land's transition from cattle to community included both personal choices and far-reaching land trades between public and private ownership.

This author had a series of 1984 and 1985 interviews with Fred Eldean, one of the prime movers in these transactions. Eldean was an investor who became president of Page Land and Cattle Co., a firm that specialized in land sales and exchanges between individuals, corporations, and federal agencies.

Eldean and his wife, Margaret, were in love with the McDowell Mountains. In the early 1950's, they would often drive east on Shea, then a roller coaster gravel trail, to the end of the road (about where the Mayo Clinic is now located). Beyond that was ranch land which was fenced and operated as the P-Bar Ranch by Bob Evans, an architect who had built the Paradise Valley Inn.

The ranch consisted of 33,000 acres with 4,540 owned by Evans and the rest leased from the government. Realizing that this part of the McDowell's east slope afforded the most beautiful views in all the Valley, Eldean bought the deeded land and the leasehold from Evans in 1954. Later, Maricopa County purchased some of the grazing rights from him for a park, but in agreeing to the sale, Eldean was granted the right to lease back any land that was not used for this purpose. This transaction created the McDowell Mountain Park.

A few years later, Eldean and others at Page Land saw that the growth of Phoenix and its suburbs would be to the north and east. With this in mind, they attempted to exchange land they held in the Sitgreaves and Coconino National Forests for some of the grazing land they were leasing for the P-Bar. The swap could not be effected, however, for the P-Bar land was owned by the Bureau of Land Management and the holdings of Page in Northeast Arizona were inside the national forests and under Department of Agriculture jurisdiction. Bureaucracy then was as tortuous as it is now, so in spite of much effort, it was impossible to get these two entities together.

To get the P-Bar leased acreage, they needed BLM land, and an alert Page employee found the way while reviewing the *Congressional Record*. She noticed that Congress had authorized land swaps across state lines if it resulted in the government acquiring private land and if it did not place any added burden on the taxpayer.

Page Land officials Bob Carlock and Eldean found that the government wanted land in Marin County, California to form a park to be called the Point Reyes National Seashore. The plans could not be completed because of an entrenched owner of 1,407 acres of land crucial to the project. Since this tract was nearly untouched since the days of Mexican occupation 200 years earlier, the government and various environmental groups were eager to protect the site.

The owner of the key acreage was Dr. Millard R. Ottinger. He did not want to sell. Eldean and Carlock engaged in months of intense negotiations with him, even renting an apartment and living nearby to assure regular contact. Finally the impasse was broken and on Jan 16, 1964, the parcel was purchased by Page. In October of 1964 an exchange of this 1,400 acres was made for about 6,800 acres of land that had been a part of the P-Bar grazing rights. This, added to the previous purchase from Evans, gave Fred Eldean and Page 11,300 acres.

The Eldean land became the Four Peaks Cattle Company. A part of the newly-acquired land was placed in the Santa Lucia Corporation, so-named because some of Page Land's European investors also had interests on St. Lucia Island in the Caribbean. In 1966, a 400-foot wide easement through their property was granted by Santa Lucia to the Arizona Dept. of Transportation for the construction of Shea Blvd. This easement involved 98 acres. Interviews in 1993 with Bob Carlock and Steve Brophy, current president of Page Land, confirmed these details.

In 1967, the McCulloch Corporation had just completed a public relations coup by purchasing the London Bridge, planning to dismantle it, with reassembly at Lake Havasu City, their development in western Arizona on the Colorado River. McCulloch was aware of the proposed Orme Dam to be built on the Verde River at its confluence with the Salt. This dam would have created a large lake upstream on the Verde. With the initial success of their Lake Havasu efforts, McCulloch was looking for other similar properties to develop.

After several months of talks with Page Land, negotiations seemed to be stalled. But then Bob Carlock took Lorne Pratt and C. V. Wood, Jr., the key McCulloch officials, on a helicopter tour of the property. This look at the stunning mountain views and the prospect of a lake at their doorstep was enough to close the deal. The eventual transaction with McCulloch was in early 1968.

The McCulloch master plan filed with Maricopa County included these tantalizing comments:

> "All of the projections of our research staff show that a 32-hour work week will be with us sometime in the 1980's. When that happens, people will be working four days a week and relaxing three days. For that reason, all our new cities are built around lakes and are recreation-oriented. We think that's important to hold the community together, to keep it a seven-day-a-week city."

The P-Bar ranch house was located at the present Fountain Hills High School parking lot site. Hank Hurlbut and his wife, Violet, lived there for three years during the late 1960's. During a recent interview, Hank said that the 3 room structure was...."a good house and the ranch was considered to be one of the better ones in the area, with dependable grass." He managed about 225 brood cows and their calves and remembered that there were numerous corrals and small outbuildings near the ranch headquarters.

The P-Bar ranch house

McCulloch used the home for its first engineering and design work, then it was rebuilt by Dick Robbins in 1976 and used as the city's first Arts and Crafts Center. Mary Read was its director for the three years of its existence. She recalls the elevated water tank that was still there and the tin roof on the ranch house. "There wasn't much else on that gravel road then," Mary said, "just a few of us interested in the arts and a lot of pack rats and coyotes. Our objective was to offer a complete spectrum of arts and crafts classes. However, the best we could manage was instruction in silversmithing by nationally-known artists Richard and Boyd Tsosie and in ceramics by Adrian Shaw."

P-Bar Ranch

Historical Society plaques

On May 17, 1997, the Fountain Hills Historical Society dedicated a monument on the high school grounds commemorating the P-Bar ranch site. Alan Cruikshank, publisher of *The Times of Fountain Hills* and Society president, arranged for the creation of two embossed, bronze plaques. One describes the significance of the location and the other bears a likeness of the ranch headquarters. Cruikshank commented: "The Historical Society is pleased to save the memory of the P-Bar ranch. As development occurs, one of our aims is to preserve the heritage of this area for future generations to remember and enjoy."

It might not be too much of a reach to conclude that Fountain Hills came into being because of the Eldean's love of the mountain views, Page Land Company's vision, a chance look at the *Congressional Record*, the government's desire for a California park, persistence in dealing with an unwilling seller, a lake on the Verde that was not to be, and a helicopter ride. What a unique scenario for the creation of a beautiful place to live!!

VERDE CATTLE AND CATTLEMEN

Until the mid 1800's, there were virtually no cattle in Arizona. The Spanish explorers brought a few head with them in the late 1500's and no doubt some of these escaped their control. Longhorn cattle from Texas drifted west and found their way to the Arizona territory but the numbers were limited, they were wild, and ownership generally rested with those who captured them.

Changes occurred following the Civil War. Veterans and displaced persons from that conflict moved west. Many had been farmers and they followed their most natural vocational pursuit. During the 1870's, herds were slowly built from seed stock brought from the east and interbred with some of the native longhorns. The first major ranches near here were in the Tonto Basin where gramma and alfilaria (filaree) grass were abundant.

The early military posts, Camp Verde, Camp Reno, Ft. Apache and Ft. McDowell were the largest customers for these cattle. It was a natural step for Tonto Basin ranchers to expand into the lower Verde Valley. Conditions here were similar but with some significant advantages. The weather was warmer, giving a longer growing season and there was a larger supply of year-round water in the rivers.

During the 1880's and 1890's, there were no restrictions on grazing and ranchers overstocked some of the best pasture land. Severe drouth in the early 80's, and again in the mid-90's accelerated the loss of vegetation. Heavy rains came near the turn of the century and caused erosion that was greater in a few years than had been experienced naturally for centuries. The carrying capacity of some ranges was reduced permanently although recent awakening to the need for conservation has restored and even improved some land.

The cattle industry was the dominant one here in the decades around the turn of the century. Business existed to serve the ranchers. There were, of course, other enterprises, notably mining and farming, but they did not provide the broad-based need for services or the dependable employment that characterized ranching.

The cowboy has been described in many ways. Much that has been written and filmed tends to glamorize the job but the cattlemen interviewed by this author didn't agree with that description. They say it was simply a tough job that required hard physical effort, many solitary hours and a willingness to adapt to any kind of weather. The cowboy was described as honest, with limited formal education but with an abundance of confidence and courage. They say that these men almost never gave their bosses any trouble and there was rarely any fighting except when they went to town and had too much to drink. For that reason, liquor was not allowed at most ranch sites.

The job most cowboys liked the least was that of shoeing horses. This was a frequent task for much of their riding was on rocky terrain and the horseshoe quality was not what it is today. These men took great pride in their work and unofficially competed among themselves as they cared for their horses and equipment. They wanted to excel, both to impress their fellow cowboys and their bosses. This spirit likely led to the concept of rodeo competition.

Cattle roundups took place in the spring and fall. It was common practice to attempt to pen the cattle near a source of water---a creek, river or spring. At these locations enclosures were constructed of wire, brush or stones. Line camps were set up near these sites when they were more than a couple of hours riding time away from ranch headquarters.

Even with the best of effort, some animals would elude the corrals and had to be pursued into the canyons and brush. They would then be roped and dragged into a relatively open area, where they could be driven along with other strays. It is hard to imagine the difficulty of herding these wild animals in the rough and rugged terrain of the McDowells or the Mazatzals.

Naturally the grazing land along the Verde was prime range and for that reason several ranchers would allow their cattle access to the same stretch of river. This was before the Tonto National Forest, before designated grazing rights and before fences or cattle guards. When spring roundup came the cowmen simply sorted out the cows by brand and put that brand on calves that were accompanying them.

The history of branding goes back thousands of years. Phoenician and Assyrian art include images of branded cattle and horses. Cattle brought from Spain to Mexico in 1522 were branded. Some brands here were first established by burning a pattern on a piece of leather, filing it with the county recorder, then staking out the ranch area by nailing similar pieces of leather to poles or trees. Since the brands were registered by county there was much duplication. The first Arizona Territory Brand Book was published in 1897 and the state has controlled this allocation since then. There is still little effort to avoid duplication of brands between states.

The spring roundup was the time of year when all ranch hands were called to action. It was the most crucial period and long days were the rule. The year's income was at stake. This occasion was also used for castrating, dehorning and cutting out the yearlings and inferior breeding stock for marketing. The fall roundups were used for selecting out the "weaners," or short yearlings, and again to cull the breeding herd.

Most cowboys did not eat a typical lunch during busy seasons. After a large breakfast at the ranch or line camp, they were in the saddle all day with only some pieces of dried fruit, beef jerky or a sandwich. Their main meal was in the evening, and it was called supper, not dinner. Top wages in the 1920's were $35 per month, plus room and board. Bronc stompers, who broke horses to ride, and any cowboy who rode the "rough string" (difficult horses) generally received an extra $10 per month.

The carrying capacity of a given range is, of course, largely dependent upon rainfall since the principal diet of cattle is native grass. It may surprise some to know that cattle also make excellent utilization of mesquite and palo verde seeds. In extremely dry years these trees generally produce an abundance of seeds---perhaps nature's way of offsetting the likely lower germination rate. It has been noticed that on ranges with plentiful native tree populations the extra energy from protein-rich seeds often more than makes up for the shortage of grass in dry seasons.

In addition to the Box Bar and P-Bar, there were other important ranchers using the lush grass of the lower Verde Valley. Pancho Monroy came here in the late 1800's, some say when soldiers were still at Ft. McDowell. He never owned land but was allowed free range. He was perhaps the first local supplier of beef to the fort.

The Adams Ranch was owned by Jefferson Davis Adams, a former Maricopa County sheriff. It was on the east bank of the Verde along Sycamore Creek. Adams Mesa, northeast of Fountain Hills, is named for this man.

The Pemberton Ranch headquarters, located in what is now McDowell Mountain Park, was said to have the best drinking water in the area and a well that was sometimes free-flowing, or artesian. However, early cowboys say its buildings were never as nice as the Box Bar or the DC Ranch of E. O. Brown.

The Brown Ranch was one of the largest. By the 1940's, it extended east to the Verde, south to present Bell Road and north almost to Carefree. The ranch home was about 2 1/2 miles north of the present Alma School/Dynamite Road intersection. The name "DC" was his abbreviation of "Desert Camp," the first name he called his spread. The name lives on now in the planned resort community on the west slopes of the McDowells.

Other prominent ranches were the Ochoa and the X-2 on the east slope of the McDowells. Ochoa watered his stock from a spring in the mountains where the Hohokam once lived, leaving petroglyphs and metate grinding holes on and in the rocks at the site. Ochoa sold his 640 acres of deeded land there for $1,000 in 1921. This became the X-2, owned by the Moores, and at one time a sister ranch to the Box Bar. Lynn Moore, operator of the X-2, hauled water from the Verde to their corrals, located near today's Rio Verde Drive and 136th Street. Later a hand-dug well, reported to be more than 100 feet deep, provided some supplemental water.

Below Horseshoe Lake, Kenneth Anderson operated the KA Ranch for many years. It is still active and known by that name. The KA is one of only two privately-owned parcels of land along the Verde from its mouth to just below Camp Verde.

One of the larger ranches in the mid-1900's was the Sears-Kay with headquarters on the road to Seven Springs northeast of Carefree. Their allotment was generally south and east of there with acreage to the crest of the Mazatzals east of the Verde. These grazing rights are now known as Sears-Club-Chalk Mountain allotment.

The Cline family grazed the slopes of Four Peaks. The Cline trailhead is at the site of their cabin along the road from the Beeline Highway to Lone Pine Saddle. Bernard Hughes later used the allotment and, more recently, John Whitney.

West of the Verde just below Needle Rock, the Cavallieres ranched in the late 1950's and early 60's. This is the same family that have been long-time Scottsdale blacksmiths. A palm tree planted in those days and the remains of stone and concrete walls are still visible at the site. The site once had the name, "Pig Farm," attached to it by local cowboys but stories of its origin are contradictory and cannot be verified.

On the southern end of the McDowells, just west of the P-Bar Ranch was the Powderhorn, owned by "Gabe" Brooks. This 160 acre homestead, just below Frank Lloyd Wright's Taliesin West, was sold in 1945 and now is a housing development with the same name.

The Goldfield Ranch, a large grazing allotment, spanned the present Beeline Highway and was just east of the Ft. McDowell Reservation. Five thousand acres of this leased land became privately owned through a land swap arranged by the Page Land and Cattle Company. It is now being developed into residential sites.

The cattle industry was an important part of early Arizona and a colorful segment of this area's history. This partial list of ranchers on the lower Verde is a reminder of the activity and impact on the desert occurring here long before the term "snowbird" was coined.

SHEEP AND THEIR BRIDGES

When Europeans came here, wild sheep were numerous and prized by Native Americans as food and for their hides and wool. Bighorn sheep and goats were frequently depicted in petroglyphs.

Coronado introduced domestic sheep to Arizona in 1540, however most of them were killed by his party for food. Some found their way into the hands of Navajos who built their herds to an estimated 1 to 1.5 million head by 1890.

In the 1870's, California had the worst drouth in its history, thus beginning the earliest Anglo introduction here as they drove their sheep to Northern Arizona in search of viable pastures. Because the activity was traditionally somewhat more fragmented than the cattle industry, the first owners were smaller and poorly organized. They tended to move on the fringes of the frontier settlements and were characterized as being content to pick up the pieces. But the sheepman always had his flock "under herd" and could move it on the hoof with little delay or expense while the cattle were widely dispersed, seldom seen by the cowboy and not easily moved to better or safer pasture.

When the first railroad, the Atlantic & Pacific, was completed across Northern Arizona in 1883, that stimulated the industry for it provided more efficient marketing for both meat and wool. The miles of ungrazed grass on the Colorado Plateau and in the Tonto Basin were inviting. Soon the flocks were growing and consolidating. By 1880, some sheepmen were as large and politically powerful as the cattlemen.

The company established by the three Daggs brothers in Flagstaff was the first in Arizona to fit this description, grazing 50,000 animals by the middle of the decade. They allowed their sheep to roam freely over the open range but complications arose as cattlemen began purchasing land that had been granted to the railroad as an inducement for them to build their tracks. Fences were erected, friction was inevitable and numerous conflicts erupted. In 1886, the Arizona Sheep Breeders and Wool Growers Association was formed, in part to allow an organized, coordinated approach to these challenges.

That same year, in the Tonto Basin just east of the Mazatzals, the Pleasant Valley War began. It became one of the most infamous confrontations between the sheep and cattle interests. Earle Forrest, in his book, *Arizona's Dark and Bloody Ground*, writes: "The Tewksburys were driving sheep over the rim of the Mogollons....the cattlemen had not wrestled this range from the ferocious Apaches only to have it taken away from them by the woolly, squirming, maggot-like creatures that every cattleman and cowboy held in contempt." *A Little War Of Our Own*, by Don Dedera, quotes the ranchers as saying: "The Tewksbury incursion could open new sheep pasturage all the way to the Salt River."

In spite of the fierce resistance of the cattlemen, the sheep growers did come into the Salt and lower Verde Valleys. They became accustomed to moving their flocks in this direction for marketing as soon as the first railroad was built into Phoenix in 1887. The high point of the industry in Arizona was 1917, when 1.5 million sheep were grazed outside Indian reservations. There has been a slow decline since then for three reasons:
1. Development of synthetic fibers
2. Immigration difficulties for Basque sheepherders
3. Rising labor costs

As the owners became familiar with conditions here, they began to use the valley not only for winter pasturage but as their headquarters. One of the last large sheep raisers in our area is the Sheep Springs Sheep Co. of Chandler, Arizona. They winter about

4000 ewes with lambing starting in October and continuing through December. Because many ewes have twins and there are some triplets, the average number of lambs saved to weaning age is about 1.3 per ewe. The lambs are weaned and marketed in April at a weight of about 100 pounds.

They trail their animals to summer pasture each May, taking 35-40 days to travel to the Greer, Arizona area. Mark Pedersen, of the Chandler company, describes their trail drives as "A mix of tradition, adventure and romance---unless the weather turns bad and then it's lots of hard work." The trek is accomplished in two groups, each with approximately 2000 sheep and traveling one day apart. Each band is herded by 2 men, 1 horse, 7 burros used as pack animals and 2 "Spanish-speaking dogs" that understand their Hispanic herders. They move 4 to 7 miles each day, allowing the flock to graze leisurely.

Dwayne Dobson, owner of the company, said, "It would be as easy and perhaps less expensive to truck the sheep to summer pasture but we continue to use the trail more out of a respect for tradition than out of necessity."

The growers that walk their flocks to summer pasture say it keeps the ewe's weight down and puts them in better breeding condition. They also become accustomed to the change in altitude gradually, thus experiencing less stress. Moving the animals avoids the weather extremes, giving them a 12-month pasture season. Sheep are also often infertile in hot climates.

In many ways, this experience evokes as much nostalgia as the great cattle drives along the Texas and Chisholm Trails. In the early drives, herders roamed over the countryside at will but---as their numbers increased and with the introduction of beef cattle in the 1880's---clashes were inevitable. The cattlemen claimed that their animals would not drink from water holes used by sheep and that sheep cropped the grass more closely. There was an added risk of wind and water erosion on rangeland that was grazed close to the ground. On the other hand, as sheep are herded over trails they tend to spread out, unlike cattle which generally create a single-file path; thus sheep are not as likely to make trails that contribute to water erosion.

In 1897, the federal government actually banned sheep from grazing public lands but continued to allow cattle. Protests from the sheepgrower's associations were able to get this policy modified in 1902.

As sheep were trailed to and from their pastures, the herders had every incentive to allow their animals to seek out the best pasturage along the way. This soon impacted on cattlemen whose ranches were located nearby. In 1916, after furious complaints, a system of driveways or trails were established and access to water holes was regulated. These generally followed the routes that had been used since the 1880's.

These trails had an inspirational effect on one perceptive observer. While he was with a flock on the Heber/Reno Driveway, famed English author, John Priestly wrote: "Arizona is geology by day and astronomy by night." This concise remark surely captures the essence of a benefit we enjoy by living here.

Sheep were required to be kept moving at least 3 miles per day on the trails. Rangers were hired by the cattlemen, with the blessing of the authorities, to enforce this movement. An 1890 report says that a ranger stationed at Cane Springs, just north of present Canyon Lake, vacated his post for a prolonged period of time. There was a mighty uproar among the ranchers, for the herders quickly allowed their flocks to spread out to gain weight. It was later discovered that the ranger's sweetheart lived up the Verde River a few miles. He had heard that a cowboy there, perhaps at the Box Bar or P-Bar, was courting her and he left to fight a romantic battle rather than policing the sheepherders.

There were two major barriers on the sheep trails in our area--the Salt and the Verde Rivers. Flocks had to swim the rivers and flow levels fluctuated drastically since there were few dams. The sheep's fleece would become waterlogged during the crossing, and it was common to lose animals to drowning and respiratory ailments due to the chilling they received. Sometimes floods would cause delays of three or more days. These events led to the construction of two sheep bridges. Each served one of the two principal trails existing at the time.

The Blue Point Bridge

BLUE POINT BRIDGE

Built in 1915 by the Arizona Wool Growers Association just 1/4 mile downstream from the present Bush Highway Blue Point Bridge, this sheep bridge served the Heber-Reno Driveway. This trail begins near Usery Pass and is about 150 miles long, crossing Sycamore Creek near Sugarloaf Mountain, passing close to old Camp Reno and terminating east of Heber.

The bridge was not well built and was replaced with a suspension structure in 1916 at a cost of $1,200. One month later, it overturned in high winds and another $600 was spent for major repairs. Rotting timbers and hard use caused its abandonment in 1927. The next replacement was 187 feet long, 21 feet above the water and used until 1966 when it was swept away by "the worst flood ever known on the Salt River."

A *Mesa Tribune* article in 1936 quoted a forest ranger as saying that 40,000 sheep used the bridge that season. An estimated total of 4 million sheep crossed at this spot.

Sheep and Their Bridges

The Verde River Sheep Bridge

VERDE RIVER BRIDGE

Jan Barstad's book, *The Verde River Sheep Bridge,* relates that there were 11,000 sheep on three grazing allotments in the Bloody Basin area northeast of Carefree in the early 1940's. In Dec. 1942, Dr. Raymond, owner of the Flagstaff Sheep Co., initiated the construction of a permanent suspension bridge across the Verde. Earlier bridges at the sites of Bartlett and Horseshoe Dams had been abandoned as the dams were built.

This structure at the Verde crossing of the Tangle Creek sheep driveway was originally called the Red Point Bridge because it is anchored on one end by vivid rust-colored volcanic rocks. The walkway was 476 feet long and 3 feet wide. The cost was $7,277, with $1,600 of this to build the road used to get trucks and supplies to the site. The first flocks crossed in the fall of 1943.

Through the years it received heavy use not only during seasonal moves but by flocks moving back and forth between the several grazing allotments along both sides of the Verde. A major ranch site with a 3-room bunkhouse, barn, caretaker's cabin, wood shed, chicken coop and shearing shed was located at the west end of the bridge. Some of the concrete slab floors are still visible there. This landmark was placed on the National Register of Historical Places in 1978. The last use was during the spring of 1979.

The Verde Bridge before reconstruction

By the mid 1980's, the bridge was in poor condition. The suspension cables were rusty and some were hanging uselessly. Many of the floor boards were missing. The Forest Service was concerned about their liability and decided to eliminate the structure. Because the bridge had provided hiker and horseback access to the Mazatzal Wilderness and because of its historic value, a major preservation effort was launched. This resulted in the demolition of the old bridge in 1988 and the building of a reproduction at the same site in 1989.

Travel to the bridge requires a rugged trip northeast from Carefree, past Seven Springs to the Tangle Creek road, then east to the Verde. A Tonto Forest map and a high-clearance vehicle is recommended. This is the last remaining structure of its type in the Southwest---a visible part of this industry's eventful history.

THE RIO VERDE CANAL

The story of the West is inevitably tied to water and the populating of this part of the country is often found to be the result of some promotion, a development or a scheme to bring people here.

Such was the plan of a group of land speculators in the late 1800's. They called themselves the Rio Verde Canal Co. and their idea was to build about 130 miles of canal from the Verde River to irrigate land between north Phoenix and the McDowell Mountains. The book, *Arizona Place Names*, states that when Frank Conkey, manager of the company first saw the valley, it was covered with spring flowers and palo verde in bloom. He named the area Paradise Valley.

The Jan. 10, 1892 issue of the *Phoenix Daily Herald* says: "Two new irrigation schemes that are of importance to this valley are now underway--the Rio Verde Canal enterprise and the Agua Fria enterprise, each of which will develop some new land on the north side that cannot be reached by the waters of the Salt River."

In Nov. of 1892, the same newspaper reports an interview with a Major Symonds, one of the heavy investors in the project. He said, in part...."In the valley lying north and east of the Phoenix mountains, which we have designated Paradise Valley, we will cover over 50,000 acres. These lands are reached by the Cave Creek Road. In that part of the Salt Valley lying between Cave Creek and the Agua Fria we will cover 60,000 more."

He was then asked, "Where are you going to get enough water to cover this immense body of land?"

"Why, my dear sir," Major Symonds replied, "the Verde drains a tract of mountain country of 6,000 square miles. We shall have one immense storage reservoir in the mountains which will hold water enough at one filling to cover 400,000 acres of land one foot deep."

When asked how he will get people here to utilize the water, Symonds said:

> "That is a matter on which we have not the slightest anxiety. Our public spirited citizens, generally, have wakened up the world to the special advantages of this locality. Only a few weeks ago, the baggage agent at Deming, North Mexico said that 'half the baggage that changes here goes to Phoenix.' There is no point more talked about in the Northeast United States than this city and the Salt River Valley. Indeed, there are no less than 75,000 people, actual residents of Phoenix and vicinity, already brought here solely through the influence of our enterprise." (A slight exaggeration since the total Phoenix population in 1900 was only 5,544--U.S. Census Bureau)

The Major's enthusiasm, we now know, was misplaced. However, some investors did participate. The Arizona Historical Foundation has water rights certificates issued in 1895 to James Watt and Andrew J. Stade, both of North Dakota. Each man signed notes for the purchase of 320 acres at $10 per acre---$3 down with an additional $1 per acre per year for the next 7 years. An 8-page contract accompanied each sale with many provisions outlining the details of how the water was to be provided.

The section of land represented by these notes is bounded today by Shea Blvd. on the north, Doubletree Ranch Road on the south, Invergordon Road on the east and 56th St. on the west.

A 32-page booklet was found that was used as promotional material by the company. It was titled *Alfalfa in the*

The Rio Verde Canal

Salt River Valley, Arizona. No publication date was shown. The opening statements, exactly as capitalized, are:

"The ranch and fruit men who speak in this pamphlet are cultivating alfalfa, raising Cattle, Hogs and Horses and growing Semi-tropical Fruits on Irrigated Lands, which were taken a few years ago at $1.25 per acre and are now worth from One to Two Hundred Dollars per acre."

Letters from 14 farmers are included and 8 pages are devoted to pictures of lush grasslands and hay crops. The booklet concludes with a page praising Arizona's climate and with the statement: "The Rio Verde Canal is now in course of construction and will be completed in the course of a year. A great deal of the land along the line of the canal is already taken up and the prospects are that it will all be taken before the canal is completed."

Certainly lots of money was lost on this venture. From the record, it seems likely that not enough land was sold at $10 per acre to convince investors to advance the large sums needed to build the canal. An 1898 notice in the *Phoenix Daily Herald* comments that the president of the company, Mr. Augustus C. Sheldon, was in England "for the purpose of interesting capital in the enterprise." It was further reported that $1.6 million dollars was required to complete the project.

As we know, the project failed but some work was actually done at the spot picked by the company's engineers. A diversion tunnel 733 feet long and 12 feet wide was built 32 miles upstream from the mouth of the Verde. A few miles of canal was dug at various locations, but no work on the dam was ever done. When Horseshoe Dam was built at this Verde River site 50 years later, the tunnel was cleared out, cement lined and used as a water diversion tunnel during the dam construction.

Had their plan succeeded, the Paradise Valley and North Scottsdale area would have been settled much more quickly. Even today there may be a trace of this ill-fated venture. Indian Bend Wash was once well-defined as it came down from the McDowell Mountains. These developers planned to join their canal with this wash near the Scottsdale/Bell Road intersection. Some dikes were built in this area and it is said that a rise in Scottsdale Road just north of the CAP canal was created by dirt excavated from a portion of the planned canal. No confirmation can be obtained.

Like the Hohokam 1000 years ago, the Rio Verde Canal Co. promoters knew the magic of water on the desert. Unlike the Salt River Project a few years later, they did not provide their vision with adequate financing and their dreams of an irrigated oasis vanished like other mirages in the hot desert sun.

ALMOST A LAKE
The Case For, And Against, Orme Dam

Many area residents may not know that Fountain Hills nearly had a lake at its east boundary. This proposal was debated for years and provides a story of conflicting interests.

After Carl Hayden's election to the U.S. Senate in 1927, he rose to become chairman of the powerful Appropriations Committee. He also became the chief sponsor of the Central Arizona Project (CAP) He had befriended the Bureau of Reclamation (BuRec) many times and when Hayden wanted CAP, BuRec was only too happy to oblige with its powerful endorsement. A well-financed lobby heavily weighted toward agri-business was with Hayden all the way.

The CAP was authorized in 1968; later that year Hayden retired, his crown jewel achieved. His successor as torch bearer became House Minority leader, Arizona Rep. John Rhodes.

The CAP project had powerful arguments in its favor:

1. The need for Colorado River water for agriculture and for the growing urban areas.
2. Control of floods.
3. More recreational boating and fishing.
4. Construction jobs at a time of high unemployment.
5. The long-time practice of taming rivers in the West, which was the rationale for forming BuRec. It was assumed to be the right thing to do.

6. McCulloch, the developer of Fountain Hills, liked the sound of a lake at their doorstep. It was one of the chief reasons they purchased the property in 1968.

In the 1970's, economic development was the driving force in Arizona and agricultural interests still held the voting power in the state legislature. There were so many powerful groups behind the entire CAP project that its total approval seemed a foregone conclusion. Added water supplies were seen as essential to keep the population boom going and flood control was a primary concern in the Salt River Valley.

The Bureau also proposed enlarging the storage capacity of the lakes behind Roosevelt, Stewart Mountain, Horseshoe and Bartlett Dams for flood control. The draft environmental statement, released by BuRec in May 1976, cost $900,000 to prepare. It was hundreds of pages and 3 1/4 inches thick. The portion of CAP that brought Colorado River water to Phoenix and Tucson got off the drawing boards quickly.

The Orme Dam, to be named for John P. Orme, one of the early founders of the Salt River Valley Water Users' Association, would have blocked the flowing water in both the Salt and Verde rivers at their confluence. Some design versions were as high as 224 feet. During early spring months, the lake level was projected to inundate about two-thirds of the Ft. McDowell Reservation. The maximum capacity would have put water over Saguaro Blvd. in Fountain Hills at some places near the golf course along that street, at the medical clinic location on El Pueblo Blvd. and the extreme northeast part of the city

The addition of a large dam at this river junction had all the advantages of the overall project and also included a "bonanza payoff" for the Ft. McDowell Indians who would be displaced-- figures from $40,000 to $75,000 per person were proposed at various times. However, this part of the project quickly became controversial.

Almost A Lake

Artist's drawing of the proposed Orme Dam

On July 7, 1976, the *Arizona Republic* reported that groups representing almost 9,000 Arizona residents had banded together to oppose Orme. The Committee To Save Fort McDowell Reservation, headed by Carolina Butler, assumed a leadership role in mobilizing environmentalists to speak out against another dam and another "taking" of Indian lands.

Yavapai tribal elder, Hiawatha Hood, summed up the feeling of most members of the reservation when he said: "Put a dollar in one hand and soil in the other, which will last for me? I can buy a new car, a color TV, some new furniture and there goes the $75,000. People say we're crazy, but we're looking to the future. We want our land. We want our language and our legends. We want our way of life. We are not for sale."

Other groups against Orme were the Maricopa and Tucson Audubon Societies, the Young Republicans Committee to Save Ft McDowell, ASU students, Salt River tubers, the Arizona Wildlife Foundation, the National Wildlife Society and the Tempe Democrats Against Orme.

A "Stop Orme Dam" T-shirt was produced in 1976 and found its way to the Smithsonian Museum for inclusion in its exhibits on political movements. The shirt featured a large picture of a bald eagle head since wildlife experts had predicted that Orme would destroy at least three bald eagle nesting sites.

On July 11, 1976, BuRec admitted they hadn't checked on possible geological faults at the Orme site. This gave its opponents new ammunition. The *Arizona Republic* reported in Sept. 1976 that the Orme dam could also jeopardize Stewart Mountain Dam by inundating the lower portion of its downstream face. The same article also told of the Ft. McDowell Indians again voting against selling their land--this time 144 to 57.

In March of 1977, Arizona's then-Gov. Castro suggested dropping Orme to save CAP. He said, in part, "CAP is viable with or without Orme." In April 1977, Pres. Carter eliminated Orme to allow continued funding for the rest of the CAP project. Opponents of the dam felt they had won the battle but the fight was far from over.

The building of the CAP canal continued and after a few months a whole set of alternatives to the original plan were revived in Congress. These were expressed in eight proposals, three of which included a dam at the original Orme site. One option was to build no additional dams but to study the safety of existing structures.

As this set of alternatives began to be researched, it was again clear that key Arizona political figures were behind an effort to revive Orme. In 1978, '79 and '80, flooding on the Salt River prompted Rep. Eldon Rudd and Burton Barr, Arizona House Majority Leader, to comment that, "An Orme Dam would have prevented the damage." Many argued that the original CAP legislation required "Orme or a suitable alternative" and the choices seemed to eventually lead back to the Orme site as essential.

Carolina Butler's committee again mobilized the opposition. A lengthy report by Valetta Canouts titled *Archaeological Survey of the Orme Reservoir* was publicized. This study noted the "great Native American cultural density and diversity" in the lower Verde valley that would be destroyed by Orme. The cost to excavate and evaluate 50% of the 130 important sites was calculated to be $22 million in 1973 dollars. The Canouts report also highlighted the widespread distribution of prehistoric canals and check dams along the lower Verde.

Dr. Robert Witzeman, President of the Maricopa County Audubon Society, said: "The lower Verde has the highest concentration of non-colonial nesting birds in the U.S. There are 195 species of birds on the Verde." Audubon's Dr. Robert Ohmart said: "Breeding bird densities on the Verde compare favorably with the highest population densities recorded in North America."

Some environmentalists and Fountains Hills citizens began referring to the "lake at our doorstep" concept, which was used in promotional material, as "mud flats at our doorstep" when they heard of the seasonal fluctuations in water levels in the proposed lake that could be as much as 140 feet.

The president of Friends of the Earth exclaimed: "The Bureau of Reclamation is like a bunch of beavers--they can't stand the sight of running water!"

The Ft. McDowell Indians, who had twice voted against Orme, insisted on a Washington, D.C. hearing and were also able to get an audience at a Geneva United Nations conference on "Indigenous People and Their Land" in Sept. of 1981. The same month, they organized a "Trail of Tears" march to the state capitol and a 10,000 meter run to publicize their opposition. They also picketed then-Sen. Barry Goldwater at one of his public appearances. Secretary of Interior, James Watt, visited Fountain Hills and met with Norman Austin, the tribal chairman.

All these efforts were noted in the press and in Washington, D.C. and proved to be persuasive. In Nov. 1981 the Orme Dam concept was formally abandoned when Plan 6 was selected. This option included a new dam, the Cliff, between Bartlett and Horseshoe on the Verde and the new Waddell Dam on the Agua Fria River. It also called for enlargement of Roosevelt and the improvement of Stewart Mountain Dam.

The *Wall Street Journal*, in a front-page story Dec. 17, 1981, expressed amazement that a small Indian tribe could stand up to the bureaucracy--and win. The Journal writer paraphrased Hiawatha Hood's comments when he said: "So to the Yavapai, the white man's money is ice, but the land is diamónds."

The Cliff Dam was later omitted from Plan 6 due to environmental and cost considerations. The Orme idea surfaced again in quoted comments by politicians in the early 80's and as recently as 1989. However, its resurrection would now require new legislation which many believe would be harder than ever to obtain.

In the 1870's and 1880's, the battles along the lower Verde River were fought with knives and bullets. One hundred years later, the battles over the Orme Dam were just as intense--and involved many more people. These more-recent battles were fought with words---and this time, the Indians won!

COOL, CLEAR WATER

Sixty-five years ago, Roy Rogers and the other original Sons of the Pioneers recorded the song, *Cool Water*, written by one of their group. The line, "Ol' Dan and I, with throats burnt dry, and souls that cry for water---cool, clear water," reminds us of its importance here. This story is a look at how a facility at our nearby river junction turns their flows into cool, clear water.

In the early 1900's, it was becoming evident that the water from Phoenix wells would not be sufficient for their needs and that its alkali and salt content was too high. The growing town recognized the value of the Salt and Verde Rivers for supplementing their supply.

In 1922, sub-surface water began to be supplied to Phoenix from several shallow wells drilled along the Verde. The above-ground line carrying the water 30 miles to downtown Phoenix was 38" in diameter and constructed of redwood slats six inches wide and 1 inch thick, held in place by metal rods. A section of this 75-year old structure is on display at the Phoenix Water Dept. offices. This design lasted only eight years before heat, dryness and bullet holes inflicted by over-enthusiastic cowboys forced its replacement with an underground concrete main that is still in use today.

After World War II, it became obvious that the system of wells would not be adequate for the rapidly-growing city. It was decided to tap the river flows. In 1948, a treatment plant was placed on the west bank of the Verde at the junction of the two rivers. The builder was the Del Webb Construction Co. This was apparently the first structure of this kind built by them before entering the residential development business. It was also the first of five similar facilities now in use by Phoenix. An expansion was finished in 1961 and in 1991 a major project added another 25%, giving it an output of 50 million gallons per day.

Phoenix considers itself fortunate in that the raw water coming into this filtration plant is of high quality. At this point the combined rivers have flowed primarily through pristine wilderness areas. Many cities take water from rivers that have passed manufacturing plants and/or major population centers, thus requiring more aggressive treatment procedures.

During normal flows the Salt is more clear than the Verde since it drains a rocky watershed. The Verde carries a larger percentage of small particles in suspension. The two river flows do not fully merge at this confluence--the different appearance of the water is evident even as far as Granite Reef Dam, two miles downstream.

Max Essex, Senior Supervisor here says, as he proudly shows this visitor around the site: "This is the choice job assignment in the system because of the remote, peaceful location." The scenery is spectacular, with exposed rocks here representing some of the oldest sedimentary strata anywhere in the area and with Red Mountain as a backdrop.

The Verde Water Treatment Plant

Cool, Clear Water

Access is from Beeline Highway along the west bank of the Verde. The road to the site, extending past the wild animal park, "Out of Africa," is a public one, but business visitors are admitted into the plant on an appointment-only basis.

Water begins its journey to the residential water tap by being pumped from the river which, at this point, includes both the Salt and Verde flows. The first stop is a sedimentation or settling basin that has the appearance of a giant marina. This basin has to be dredged occasionally to remove the silt. This material is then used to build up the banks of the river.

Water is pumped from here to the highest part of the facility. Gravity then moves it through a process that includes the addition of a flocculation agent to cause the remaining small particles in suspension to settle. After moving through a coagulation and clarification basin, the clear water enters a filtration gallery where it passes through anthracite coal and sand. Chlorine is added if necessary. At all stages of the process, EPA standards for clarity and purity are met or exceeded. Sampling from seven locations and a bank of three computer screens monitor every stage of the process. There is also an on-site analytical laboratory.

Gravity sends the finished product to a point just west of Gilbert Road. There, booster pumps transfer the water to a large reservoir at 64th St. and Thomas for distribution to city mains. Similar storage facilities throughout the city can hold a total of about 450 million gallons. The largest demand day through the end of 1996 was August 7, 1995 when 432 million gallons were used.

The Phoenix Water Dept. operates as a business enterprise and is supported by revenues, not taxes. Their water rates, when compared with the 20 largest cities in the nation, ranked 13th in 1996.

The next time we admire Red Mountain or cross the Verde on Beeline Highway we can remember that the business of producing "cool, clear water" is going on around the clock, 7 days a week, at this scenic river junction.

TWO RIVERS RUN BY US

In the state of Arizona, few rivers have year-round flowing water. The Fountain Hills area has proximity to two--the Salt and the Verde. This adds another dimension to our locale with tubing, fishing, boating and priceless riparian wildlife habitat close by.

There are some similarities between the two rivers--their flows are controlled by Salt River Project (SRP) and their watersheds are close in size, about 6,500 square miles each. However, the rest of the story is one of contrast.

NAMES

Coronado's troops called the Salt River, "Rio de las Balsas" (The River of the Rafts). At various times it was "Azul," "Prieto," "Rio de la Assuncion," "Rio Compuesto," "Salado" and "Rio Salinas." The Pima Indians called it "Onk Akimel," from two of their words meaning "salty" and "river."

In April 1925, the *Arizona Republic* newspaper reported that the Phoenix Chamber of Commerce was circulating a straw ballot to test the feelings of the population toward changing the name of the Salt River. Some felt that the name connoted dryness, bitterness and brackishness which were not the proper terms to attract tourists to the valley. No formal changes were made because of this effort although the term "Valley of the Sun" gradually became accepted and is used along with "Salt River Valley."

The Verde was once called the "Rio Alamos" for the cottonwood trees so common along its banks and later it was "El Rio de los Reyes" (The River of Kings). Trappers and scouts in the

1800's called it the "San Francisco" since they thought its headwaters were in those mountains. The present name came from the Spanish Beltran/Espejo expedition in 1583 when they came west from New Mexico Territory and reveled in the green vegetation lining the banks.

VOLUME

The upper portion of the Salt, in the White Mountains of eastern Arizona, is at an elevation of 10-11,000 feet. The Verde headwaters, in the Juniper and Bill Williams Mountains, are at about 7,500 feet. This elevation difference translates into 40 inches of moisture on the upper Salt and 20 on the Verde, giving the Salt 62% of the combined flow.

DAMS

There are four on the Salt above the confluence of the rivers and two on the Verde. All hold water during high-flow periods for irrigation needs downstream. This is the only function of the Verde dams, but the four on the Salt also have power generating ability. For this reason, the Salt dams are managed to be at near capacity just before the summer months so their releases can provide electricity for SRP during the heavy demand period.

STORAGE CAPACITY

There is a marked difference in the storage on the two rivers. Total capacity is almost 2.9 million acre feet (one acre of water one foot deep). The Salt has 89%--the Verde 11%.

Roosevelt Lake is the major difference, with the recent expansion giving it 76% of the combined total. Its newly-created flood control space of 556 thousand acre-feet is included in this figure.

TRIBUTARIES

The Black and White Rivers join near Ft. Apache to form the Salt. Tonto Creek is the Salt's largest feeder stream.

The East Verde has the most inflow to the Verde, joining it west of Payson.

PEAK FLOWS

In spite of the heavier volume on the Salt, the Verde flow is more erratic. The largest variations occurred during the flood years of 1978, 1980, 1991 and 1993. This could be partially due to a larger percentage of the Salt volume coming from more gradual snow melt. On the Verde, with a higher portion of the total coming from rain, the runoff is almost immediate. The most important reason is that the Verde watershed is oriented in a north-south direction. Most heavy winter storms move in a west to east direction, thus dropping water quickly on the entire Verde valley but only gradually on the Salt.

It must also be realized that there just isn't that much space to store water on the Verde. This was one of the principal arguments used by the proponents of the Orme Dam.

SENSORS

In the Salt watershed there are 10 sensors measuring the depth and moisture levels of snow--in the Verde area there are 5. In the Salt and its branches there are 13 stream flow gauges--in the Verde there are 18. At each dam there is a water depth sensor. All of these relay data at least every 4 hours and may be programmed to report every 15 minutes. At 8 of these locations there is a separate, redundant station for emergency use.

Data from these sensing devices and from weather satellite and forecasting services are monitored on several screens at the sophisticated SRP control center where decisions are made on water releases from all six dams.

WATER QUALITY

Salt outcroppings above the Salt River Canyon near the mouth of Carrizo Creek gave this river its appropriate name. Its salinity is about twice that of the Verde. The Salt is also higher in dissolved solids, likely due to its more rocky stream bed.

There is more suspended sediment in the Verde. The difference in clarity is often visible at the confluence of the rivers. This occurs because the lower Verde flows through alluvial soil while the Salt is generally confined to rock-lined canyons. There are also twice as many dams on the Salt, allowing more settling-out of particles.

The water quality of both rivers has been steady to slightly improved in the last two decades.

SOIL FERTILITY

A map prepared in 1866 shows the Verde Valley as "Rich bottom land---much grass" and the Rio Salinas as "Very rocky." Today, this still seems an apt description since the Verde has several locations where there is fertile land that responds well to irrigation.

*****

Dallas Reigle, Senior Hydrologist at SRP, was an important research source for this subject. Water quality information was supplied by the U. S. Geological Survey Office.

Although two rivers run by us, they are not the same. Each one is a magnificent, renewable asset. Their careful management can assure our future in this unique location.

OUR "DAMMED" RIVERS

Six nearby dams, managed by the Salt River Project (SRP), control water flow on our rivers. They provide a variety of services to the general public. Though we seldom consider it, our lives are significantly affected by their presence. Let's take a look at each of them.

ROOSEVELT

This was the first of the SRP dams to be completed. It created what was then the largest man-made lake in the world, at a cost of $10.3 million and the lives of 30 workers. This dam became a National Historic Landmark in May 1963 because of its unique construction, called "cyclopean, rubble-masonry, thick arch." It is the highest masonry arch dam in the world and was one of the last of this type to be built. In March 1911, Pres. Theodore Roosevelt was present at the dedication of this structure named for him.

A major expansion was completed in 1996, increasing the height of the dam 77 feet and doubling the maximum capacity of the lake. The modification kept the core intact and is called a concrete gravity arch. Fifteen feet of this new space was dedicated to water storage and 62 feet for flood control, the first available for this purpose on either the Salt or Verde Rivers. The new bridge constructed as a part of the renovation is 1,080 feet, the longest two-lane, single-span, steel arch bridge in North America. Extensive recreational facilities were also added, including 1,500 new campsites, 80 picnic sites, nine boat launches, six fish cleaning stations and the world's largest solar-powered campground. It also has a reputation as the best fishing lake in the SRP group.

Roosevelt Dam after the 1996 expansion

HORSE MESA

This dam created Apache Lake and is named for a nearby mesa where horse thieves once hid stolen herds. It is the second largest lake in the SRP system. Several campgrounds and a marina offer a variety of recreation facilities.

MORMON FLAT

This was the second dam to be built, forming Canyon Lake. It was named for the pioneers from Utah who stopped nearby to camp enroute to the Mesa area. All of the three lower Salt River dams use a concrete thin-arch style of construction.

The smallest of the SRP lakes, it still provides numerous campground sites and full marina and boating services. Apache and Canyon Lakes can be reached only by traveling on the Apache Trail (State Highway 88).

STEWART MOUNTAIN

This dam was named for the mountain that is just 1 1/2 miles northwest. The lake formed by this structure is Saguaro. Closest to the Phoenix area, it is the one most heavily used for recreational purposes. It is the lowest major dam on the Salt, just 10 miles from its merger with the Verde.

Saguaro Lake is the busiest of the SRP lakes. The light colored cliffs in the right background are volcanic tuff, further described on page 134.

HORSESHOE

This Verde River dam was named for the U-shaped bend in the river at the site. It was built as a result of a unique agreement between SRP and the Phelps Dodge Corporation. In order to obtain water from the Black River in eastern Arizona for its mining operations there, Phelps Dodge agreed to totally finance the structure. This Black River source of water is located on the San Carlos Indian Reservation and in 1997 was the subject of tense negotiations that threatened the supply of water to the Phelps Dodge mine in Morenci, Az.

The spillway gates were added three years after the dam was finished and were funded by the city of Phoenix, giving them added water rights. Like Bartlett, it does not have power generating ability. Horseshoe Lake is often the first to be drained during extended dry periods. It is an earthen and rock-fill structure.

BARTLETT

This downstream dam is twenty-one river miles above the river's mouth. It was named for Bill Bartlett, a government surveyor active during its planning and construction period. Unlike the Salt River dams, which were totally financed by SRP, this one received 20% of the construction funds from the Bureau of Indian Affairs. It is a multiple-arch structure. At the base the concrete arch thickness is 7 feet and at the top 2 feet.

Our "Dammed" Rivers

Bartlett Dam

STATISTICS:

Dam	Roosevelt	Horse Mesa	Mormon Flat	Stewart Mountain	Bartlett	Horseshoe
Lake Name	Roosevelt	Apache	Canyon	Saguaro	Bartlett	Horseshoe
Completed	1911	1927	1926	1930	1939	1946
Dam Height (ft.)	357	300	224	208	283	194
Dam Length (ft.)	1,210	660	380	1,260	800	1,500
Surface Acres	21,500	2,600	950	1,280	2,700	2,800
Capacity (000's acre-feet)	1,653*	245	58	70	178	131
Max. Water Depth (ft.)	249	264	142	119	188	126
Shoreline (miles)	128	42	28	22	33	27

*does not include flood control space

When the first trappers, miners, cattlemen and farmers came to our valley, the Salt and Verde Rivers would sometimes flood savagely, then ebb to a trickle during the dry seasons. Water, the life-blood of the desert, was either not available or there was too much. As in much of the West, a growing population was not likely until a dependable source of water for irrigation was assured. The dams also provided a continuous stream-flow, generated electricity and made water recreation of all kinds available. It's likely that without these dams, many of us would be living elsewhere.

GRANITE REEF DAM

Other chapters have discussed our two major rivers and the Salt River Project dams that store water on both of them. We also live close to another dam that is seldom seen by the public and gets little notice. Yet this dam, Granite Reef, is a crucial part of the Salt River Valley's water delivery system.

About 1,500 years ago, the prehistoric persons we now call the Hohokam learned how to coax river water onto the banks and, by cleverly using every slight degree of elevation difference, to distribute this life-giving liquid over many acres. As they perfected their techniques and opened up new acreage for irrigation, their nutrition improved, life spans increased and population grew.

One of their concerns had to have been how to assure themselves of a year-round supply of water to sustain the flow through the irrigation ditches. Then, as now, river flows were intermittent. Flooding and drouth surely must have provided a challenge for them. We also know that river channels change and that a canal heading that was ideal at one time might be inadequate a year later---perhaps, even a few weeks later.

Check dams were used by the Hohokam to divert water into their canals. Archaeologists have found numerous bits of evidence verifying this technique. The materials usually employed were limbs and large stones for the base of the structure, augmented by brush, dirt and gravel.

Granite Reef Dam

When Jack Swilling and his associates began clearing out the Hohokam canals to found the village that would become Phoenix, they learned that much of the work had to be done at the canal headings. As the river had changed its course over the centuries, it was either too far away or its channel was cut too low to permit water to flow freely into the old canals. The Mormon Lehi party found the same thing in 1877 when they crossed the Salt and began working on the south bank canals.

These early pioneers persevered, however, and with enormous effort they maintained their newly-cleared canals, dams and canal headings. They, like the Hohokam, found a need for frequent repair of their diversion dams. As early as 1879, *Phoenix Daily Herald* editor, Charles E. McClintock, commented on the difficulty of maintaining flow from the Salt River into the canals then in use. He wrote "....The solution is to build a solid rock and cement dam that will be strong, durable and tight, down to the bed rock, and from bank to bank."

By the last decade of the century, population in the Salt Valley was increasing. In February 1891, an unprecedented flood again damaged or destroyed the fragile dams and canal headings. A series of drouth years followed. Influential farmers clamored for action and the business community, realizing that agriculture was now the most important enterprise here, quickly supported all efforts to improve the situation.

Many sources of outside capital investment were investigated. A previous chapter described the efforts of the Rio Verde Canal Company. Another promising attempt was made by the Hudson Reservoir and Canal Company. They hoped to build at the site that would become Roosevelt Dam and to build a diversion dam just below the Salt/Verde confluence. Despite each company spending hundreds of thousands of dollars they were unable to interest enough private investors to complete their plans.

Local business and agricultural interests then focused their attention on the issuance of bonds as a method of financing. Although this approach seemed feasible, nothing tangible was accomplished by the end of the century.

The Hansbrough-Newlands Act, enacted into law in 1902, provided the means to the desired action. Benjamin Fowler, a recently-arrived book publisher from the East Coast and now an Arizona legislator, became the chief lobbyist in Washington to assure the valley's participation in this new legislation, which placed the responsibility for irrigation of land in the West in the hands of the Department of the Interior.

Theodore Roosevelt, the new President of the United States, was an advocate of public assistance for irrigation in the West. It was felt at the time that the public lands here would be made more productive and profitable by populating them with the homeless and unemployed from the eastern cities. Irrigation would hopefully open thousands of small farms to accomplish this objective.

The most important factor causing the early government involvement here was the willingness of the Salt River Valley farmers living south of the river to pledge their land as collateral, assuring repayment of expenditures needed to build a dam. The Salt River Water Users Association was formed on March 14, 1903, setting the framework for this landmark event. The key men in accomplishing the enormous organization task were: Benjamin Fowler, George Maxwell, John P. Orme and Dwight B. Heard.

The first move was to begin construction of a large dam at "....the best site available in the Western United States," where Tonto Creek joined the Salt. This was to be the largest undertaking until that time in the Arizona Territory. It must be remembered that this was still 9 years away from the date of Arizona statehood. Phoenix population was only 5,544 in 1900 and all of Maricopa County was only about 20,000 persons.

A semi-transient alliance of north side farmers, the Arizona Water Company, had completed the Arizona Dam about one mile downstream from the Verde/Salt confluence in 1885. This dam, which diverted water to north side canals, had repeatedly been washed away or damaged by floods. It also was a problem for the newly-formed Salt River Water Users Association. The Department of Interior was now building Roosevelt Dam and its cost was to be repaid by south side farmers. A way had not been found to resolve allocation of water between competing north/south farming interests.

Just as the Roosevelt Dam construction was beginning, winter floods in late 1905 and early 1906 washed out the Arizona Dam again. The destruction of the dam at this time forced the issue. The north side farmers were having trouble finding the money to rebuild. The government would not build a replacement dam without an agreement in place to repay the costs, similar to their Roosevelt Dam agreement.

The issue was resolved in July 1906, when the Department of Interior grudgingly agreed to buy the Arizona Water Company assets and to rebuild the diversion dam. These expenditures were added to the costs that would eventually be repaid to the government by the Water Users Association.

The new structure was begun in Oct. 1906, while Roosevelt was still under construction. It was below the old site of the Arizona Dam, just south of Red Mountain, and was to be called Granite Reef. The name is derived from a rocky promontory that extends out into the river. This ridge continued underneath the river and provided a solid bedrock foundation for the structure. This barrier would build a reliable water level allowing diversion into canals on both the north and south sides of the river.

A multi-exposure picture, pieced together to form a panoramic view of the construction site, gives an extraordinary look at how remote this area was in the first decade of this century. The shots were taken from a bluff about 1/4 mile south and east of the dam. Except for the construction structures, no other evidence of civilization is in view. With a magnifying glass, about 10 Indian huts are visible upstream, indicating that they, too, were working on the dam.

The *Phoenix Gazette* in its July 6, 1908 edition, says: "The Granite Reef camp....is one of the best regulated in the territory. The men have enjoyed the luxury of daily mail service, lights and a complete system of waterworks with showerbaths in connection....There have been times when intoxicating liquors were smuggled into camp, but it was with the result of a swift conviction...."

There was a Y-shaped mess hall with wings where White and Hispanic workers ate separately. Common laborers were paid $2 per day but skilled workers and foremen received $3-5. Five men died during the 20-month construction period. The mayor of Mesa declared a public holiday on June 13, 1908, when the Granite Reef Dam was dedicated. Water was diverted into the Arizona Canal amid the cheers of thousands. The *Phoenix Gazette* editorialized as follows:

> "The entire Salt River Valley rejoices as one man today.....It rejoiced when it learned that the Tonto (Roosevelt) Dam was to be constructed and when it was announced that a permanent diversion dam was to be constructed....But now the latter dam has been completed. It is no longer a possibility but a reality which will be self evident when the next flood comes down the Salt River. Nothing to equal in enthusiasm and splendor....attending the connection of the Granite Reef Dam with the Arizona Canal has ever before been seen in this valley, and probably will not be seen again...."

Excursions to the new dam were so popular that the *Gazette* reported, "Mesa capitalists are planning to establish a hotel and pleasure resort there." The pages of both Mesa and Phoenix newspapers contained frequent notices of families and groups "....going to Granite Reef for a day's outing of boating, fishing and picnics."

Granite Reef Dam in recent years

Earl Merrill's *Mesa Tribune* columns, written in the early 1970's, and Salt River Project publications have helped piece together this story of nearly a century ago. Granite Reef, little noticed by the public, keeps on providing a dependable supply of irrigation water to hundreds of customers in the Salt River Valley.

SUPERVISOR JIM HART
Father Of The Beeline

Just 1.6 miles east of the Shea Blvd./Beeline Highway intersection there are 4 monuments on the south side of the highway. Have you noticed them? Have you stopped?

The text on this plaque is:
A Memorial to
James G. Hart
1908
1960
One of Arizona's Trail Blazers
This highway is, in part,
his inspiration and monument.
Member Maricopa Co.
Bd. Of Supervisors
1953 to 1960
(The bottom line is unusual
and symbolically says,
"Bee-line to Heart line")

The Hart monument existed on the south side of the Beeline at the Shea intersection for 22 years. During the upgrading of that intersection, the monument was moved to the northwest corner.

In 1993, it was moved to its present site and joined by three other memorials. One commemorates Camp Reno and was erected by the John H. Page Land Co., another Dr. Carlos Montezuma (Wassaja), erected by the Arizona Highway Dept. and the third refers to Ft. McDowell and was placed by the Arizona Department of Transportation.

Monuments on the south side of Beeline Highway

In the early 1950's, there were only three Maricopa County Supervisors. Jim Hart was one of them. Many were pressing for an improvement of the route between Phoenix and Payson. According to Board of Supervisor minutes, none was more ardent than Jim Hart. He had owned a summer home in Payson since 1950 and was eloquent in his presentation of the reasons for an improved road.

Hart was born in Bentonville, Arkansas on Aug. 9, 1908. He graduated from high school in Pittsburg, Kansas in 1925, attended Pittsburg Business College for 1 year, then came to Phoenix with his parents where he worked as a plant foreman for Reynolds Aluminum. He saw action in combat zones in Europe during World War II and was wounded in action.

He became a civic worker, real estate man and the first Republican to serve as a supervisor in more than 30 years when he was elected in late 1951 as a member of the "better government team." Known as an exceptionally good supervisor, he took pride in personally answering every phone call he received from his constituents.

Fred Glendenning, retired County Engineer and Oscar Lyon, retired State Engineer recalled for this writer that in the early 1950's the most direct route from the valley to Payson was a rough, unpaved road from Mesa to Saguaro Lake, then north and east. At best, the trip from the valley to the mountains was an arduous one. This route had been completed in 1933 and called the Bush Highway, named for Harvey Bush, a prominent Mesa civic leader and lumberman.

Negotiations with the Salt River-Pima and Ft. Mc.Dowell tribes for a diagonal highway right-of-way were authorized on May 14, 1953 by the Board of Supervisors. At that time the new highway was referred to in their minutes as the "Phoenix-Payson Highway," and the "Bee-Line Highway."

The new Beeline began from the eastward extension of Mc Dowell Road, following its present route to intersect with the Bush Highway at the present Saguaro Lake turnoff. At the same time, the route on to Payson was upgraded in many places as the curves were smoothed in anticipation of faster speeds and heavier traffic.

The federal government was able to help with forest highway funds. The state wanted the road upgraded but didn't have the money to do it. They agreed to re-survey the route and take over the maintenance of the road if Maricopa County would come up with money to match the federal aid. The route was opened in 1958.

On Feb. 6, 1960, Hart spent the day in Payson discussing a real estate deal with Bob Herberger of Scottsdale and Dan Gainey of Owatonna, Minnesota. Gainey is also known as the owner of a former Arabian horse ranch on Scottsdale Road, now the Gainey Ranch resort. Herberger is a member of the family for whom the downtown Phoenix theater is named.

At 6 p.m. Hart left Payson to return to Phoenix. Near the present Shea/Beeline intersection his car left the road on the right side, came back across the highway, crossing a cattle guard, then left the road on the left side, finally striking an ironwood tree. He was apparently killed instantly on the highway he worked so hard to upgrade. Another irony was noticed immediately. Mr. Hart was scheduled to attend a highway safety conference called by the County Supervisors the day after his burial.

Jim Hart

Both the *Phoenix Gazette* and the *Arizona Republic* called Hart the "Father of the Beeline" and commented that its construction was due more to his efforts than any other one person. The State Treasurer proposed that the name of the highway be changed to the James Hart Highway.

One Board of Supervisors member said: "Our state will miss him, for his work to clean up Maricopa County has been of utmost importance." The newspapers commented that Hart was instrumental in establishing both the county parks and health departments.

In Payson, efforts were started to create a memorial for Mr. Hart by purchasing a much-needed piece of hospital equipment for the Payson Hospital. It was to have borne a copper plate inscribed "In Memory of Jim Hart, our friend." The donations were later redirected to help fund the Beeline memorial.

Take a look next time you pass this monument site. There's a wide shoulder providing a place to park and update yourself on some of the abundant history of our area.

THAT EVENING GLOW IS "TUFF"

One of the best times to enjoy the spectacular views in the lower Verde Valley is when sunset is near and the mountain ranges to the east delight us with a variety of changing colors and shadings. One of the most striking parts of this panorama is the golden glow that is present on many parts of the mountains southeast of Fountain Hills. What causes this?

About 20-30 million years ago, the area to the southeast was subjected to violent volcanic eruptions. As multiple flows of molten lava reached the surface, gigantic cavities were created underground. Subsequently, the weight of surface deposits caused a collapse into these caverns.

During the latter part of this era, tremendous volcanic explosions produced millions of tons of fractured rock and smaller fragments. This material had a high gaseous content and spread out laterally as an enormous, red-hot dust cloud moving along the ground for miles in all directions. Many of these eruptions resulted in deposits that covered the terrain to a depth of up to 2,000 feet. Although not a product of combustion, this material is often called volcanic ash.

Some of these explosive deposits became solidified into rock by minerals in surface water and the weight of subsequent overlays of erosional material. Other eruptions were plastic enough to flow into lower areas and, upon cooling, become partially or wholly welded together. Stone from both these sources is called "tuff."

That Evening Glow is "Tuff"

Most volcanic rocks are darker, have a higher density and are associated with lava eruptions and flows. Their color is generally derived from a high content of iron and magnesium-bearing minerals.

Tuff can be composed of a variety of minerals. It is generally rough to the touch since it contains partly sorted, sharp-cornered dust particles. The lighter colored stone is called rhyolite or dacite. A singular property is that its hard, flat-sided particles give it a glassy appearance and a reflective capability.

The bright rhyolite tuff layers in the Usery and Goldfield Mountains and in the Superstition Wilderness have a yellowish-tan color and contain a significant amount of quartz particles, producing the distinctive glow that is so evident in the late afternoon sun. Some of these formations are horizontal and some have been tilted as uplifting occurred.

Early explorers and Indians referred to some of these layers as "soapy stone," believing it to be a high water mark left by massive prehistoric flooding. A striking example of this mistaken supposition is visible while driving northeast on the Beeline Highway from McDowell Road to about the Gilbert Road intersection. A light yellow, horizontal stripe can be seen near the top of one of the mountains to the east. The Wind Cave Trail in Usery Park leads to a wind-eroded cavern that has been formed in this layer of tuff. Some early Spaniards actually used the term "mountain of foam" when referring to these deposits. These colloquial references to tuff are understandable since it is typically a more porous stone with less density.

The range to the immediate east of Red Mountain is called the Usery Mountains. Few of the thick tuff deposits here or in the Superstition Wilderness are exposed to a Fountain Hills view. Between these two, the Goldfield Mountains contain many cliffs of nearly pure tuff. These are the ones that are dramatically colored by the afternoon sun and the most visible from Fountain Hills. They are located on the south side of the Salt River and just downstream from Saguaro Lake. To obtain a closer view of them drive east on Bush Highway past the Usery Pass intersection and the Blue Point Bridge on a sunny afternoon. The light colored layer in the picture of Stewart Mountain Dam and Saguaro Lake on page 122 is seen by many and is a good example of this material.

Some tuff deposits are named for the Greek volcano, Santorini. Others commemorate the Vesuvius eruptions that buried Pompeii and Herculaneum in Italy in 79 AD. A famed writer, Pliny the Elder, was aboard a ship that was close to the eruption. When he saw the towering ash and smoke cloud he demanded that the ship be sailed into the Pompeii harbor in spite of the protests of the crew. Nearly all suffocated as the ash covered everything to a depth of several feet. His nephew, Pliny the Younger, recorded this account as a part of his prolific writings. Geologists now refer to layers like those at Pompeii as "Plinian air-fall deposits."

The tuff deposits we see from here are known as the Geronimo Head Formation. We can be thankful that these cliffs in the Goldfield Mountains have the reflective ability to turn the late afternoon sun into a golden glow that highlights and enhances our views to the southeast.

PHON D. SUTTON/COON BLUFF

Have you wondered about these unusual names for two Bush Highway recreational sites on the south bank of the Salt River near its confluence with the Verde?

PHON D. SUTTON

The Sutton spot bears the name of a man with a birthday on May 1, 1898. This day is an important one in our country's history---the date of Admiral George Alphonso Dewey's stunning naval victory in the Spanish-American War battle of Manila Bay. The crucial naval maneuvers performed by Admiral Dewey allowed the American fleet to destroy the 10-ship Spanish flotilla without the loss of a single American sailor or ship. It was the event that turned the tide for the Americans in the Phillipines.

A boy born that day in Pennsylvania was named Alphonso Dewey Sutton in honor of Admiral Dewey. He was never called Alphonso, except perhaps by his parents at an early age. He preferred "Phon" and was always known by that nickname.

He moved to Mesa, married there and became a lineman for Southside Gas and Electric Company, now Pinnacle West. He later opened his own electrical store and became a prominent businessman in Mesa. His name appears in the *Mesa Tribune* several times during the 1930's as chairman of different fund drives for charitable projects.

He and others from Mesa became concerned about environmental issues long before this was a popular crusade. They noticed that some riparian property was coming under the control of a few pioneer families who understood its importance. His group, although never formally organized, became influential with state legislators and power brokers as they watched for opportunities to facilitate the acquisition of property from estates. They would then work to get them returned to public ownership.

Phon D. Sutton

In 1959, Phon Dewey Sutton died and in his honor the Forest Service officials decided to name this site for him. It had previously been called "Forks of the River."

In 1985, the Tonto National Forest and the student chapter of the Arizona State University Wildlife Society cooperated in the construction of an interpretive trail through the Sutton area. Much of the work was done by students with funds coming from the Arizona Game and Fish Dept. This trail has since been badly damaged by flooding but will hopefully be rebuilt. Phon Sutton's son is living in Gilbert and helped with this information.

COON BLUFF

Coon Bluff got its name through a humorous occasion that occurred about 1919. Lehi Boy Scout leaders, Rollin Jones and Roy Sirrine, planned a summer overnight camping trip to a spot on the Salt River about halfway between Granite Reef Dam and the Blue

Point Bridge. The group went out on a Friday afternoon. During that night Sirrine caught a large raccoon in a trap he'd set along the river.

The next morning, the raccoon was the talk of the camp and the subject of a lively discussion about its fate. Some of the boys remembered that several of their parents were coming out to have a noon meal with them, spend the afternoon and take them home. With glee and anticipation, it was decided to use the 'coon as the main course for the lunch to be shared with their parents.

Some said the animal became a part of a stew, and some remembered that the meat was roasted, but all agreed the main course---which was represented to their parents as pork---was delicious. Naturally, the boys giggled their way through the meal and loved the fact that they were putting one over on their elders. For weeks after, the deception was the topic of conversation. The secret lasted until inevitably, some boy let the truth slip out.

The scouts adopted this spot as their favorite camping place and, of course, began calling it Coon Camp, Coon's Point or Coon Bluff. In 1936 the *Mesa Tribune* said that, "Tonto Forest rangers have installed swings, fireplaces and tables at Coon Bluff. The site is now completed for public use."

A Tonto National Forest map dated 1946 does show a "Coon Bluff" at that spot and a Standard Oil map printed in 1948 shows the location as "Coon's Bluff." Earl Merrill, columnist for the *Mesa Tribune*, provided these details in a 1968 story.

It isn't often that a Boy Scout prank gets memorialized with an official national forest designation. It is a piece of history that can be recalled next time you drive by on Bush Highway.

PURPLE MOUNTAIN MAJESTIES

Four Peaks provides us with wondrous sunset displays of lilac, violet and purple hues. But it also has supplied us, and the world, with another, more tangible, purple treasure---high quality amethyst crystals.

For centuries, amethyst has been considered the royal gem because of its color. Purple was the emblem of rank or authority and the color most often associated with European monarchs.

Spanish history reportedly shows the discovery of a Four Peaks lode in the 18th century and significant shipments of these gems to the homeland where they found their way into crown jewels of five countries.

It is known that a prospector named Jim McDaniels did re-discover the deposit about 1900. He was following a quartz "float," usually a good precursor to gold. Instead he found the canyon floor littered with purple crystals. Gold and silver were the only objectives of most prospectors in those days so the site was merely noted and left untouched.

The ancient Greeks believed that if they drank wine from a cup carved from amethyst they would not become intoxicated. They named this beautiful purple quartz with a combination of the Greek words for "not" and "to intoxicate." In addition to these legendary powers, it is also the birthstone for February.

Another story from Greek mythology tells that Bacchus, the God of Wine, swore to turn the next person he saw into a tiger. Amethyst was the name of a beautiful maiden on her way to worship at the shrine of Diana, the huntress. Diana magically turned Amethyst colorless to protect her. Bacchus still saw her, but relented and poured wine over her, thus the purple color and another reason for the name of this beautiful crystal.

The location of the amethyst mine is at one of the most remote and rugged parts of the Mazatzal Mountains. We can identify the site because of the extensive mining activity that took place there in the last 50 years. The location is best seen with binoculars and is between the two southern-most peaks. After finding the "V" between these peaks, drop down slightly to see the mine's waste rock slope. The best time for viewing is in the late afternoon or after snow has fallen on the peaks. In either case the relative smoothness and lack of trees on the slope distinguishes the spot from the surrounding rugged, brushy area. The mine site itself is at the top of the grade, only 300 feet below and slightly to the right of the notch between the two peaks.

The mine's waste rock slope can be seen clearly in this aerial view of Four Peaks

The *Mineralogical Record* of Mar.-Apr., 1976 describes the process by which these crystals were formed, "The amethyst of this deposit occur in linings of voids in faults of the Mazatzal quartzite.

The voids were intermittently filled with hot liquid solutions from intrusions below. Successive stages of quartz deposition occurred, as evidenced by alternating concentric rings of colorless quartz, hematite and amethyst around the angular fragments."

The purple color that enhances the quartz is caused by the presence of manganese in these hot solutions that flooded the cavities in the uplifted peaks millions of years ago. The more valuable, darker colors reflect a higher manganese content. The value is also dependent upon its clarity, or lack of foreign material in the solution as it was being deposited.

Amethyst does occur elsewhere in the state but not in the quality or quantity that has been discovered here. Arizona is probably the only state in the U.S. which produces gem quality stones, according to Ken Phillips, Chief Engineer for the Arizona Department of Mines and Mineral Resources. He further says, "The best amethyst from the Four Peaks mine is considered to be as good as that found anywhere in the world."

Another reference book, *Mineralogy in Arizona*, states, "Superb gem-quality amethyst of a rich, red-violet color was produced from the Four Peaks mine and rivals the best Siberian material, which is the standard of the gem trade."

Blasting with dynamite is not an option, since it would shatter the crystals. Hand tools must be used. It is a slow and tedious extraction method. The only access to the site is by helicopter or by long, very difficult trails. For many of the active mining years helicopters were used to bring in workers and supplies and take out crystals. For about 18 months 4 mules were used to replace the helicopter, trudging over trails to the nearest forest road.

There have been several owners. Even though the amethyst vein was producing high quality crystals, problems were plentiful, most of them attributed to the rugged wilderness location of the mine.

About May of 1925, Mrs. Gertrude Evelin of Phoenix sold the mineral claim on this 20 acre parcel of land to Louis and Rudolf Juchem, brothers who were stone cutters from Germany but then living in Los Angeles. A mining publication of that time reported the price as $2,500 to be paid at $50 per month. It was also stated that they wanted no publicity on the sale. The land was patented to private ownership in 1942. They called their mine the Arizona Amethyst Placer.

In 1955 when they filled out their annual report to the Arizona Mining Commission, the Juchem Brothers said that the minerals produced there were "amethyst crystals" and "axle grease mica." They also stated that the mine would be for sale soon due to health problems in the family.

Mr. Al W. Storer and his wife, Cecile, purchased the mine in 1963 and worked it for many years. Speculation in mining publications at the time put the sale price at $50,000. The Storers operated the Rock Hobby Shop in Phoenix, the House of Amethyst gem shop in Scottsdale and later, in Fountain Hills.

During the late 1960's and 1970's, a helicopter delivered supplies to the miners who generally stayed on site, returning to the Valley only on week-ends. The crystals were carried out on the return trips. A corrugated iron shack was built near the helicopter pad as an equipment shed and to provide shelter for the miners as needed. The terrain was so steep that the downslope portion of the building had to be supported by poles about 15 feet long. This shed could clearly be seen from Fountain Hills and Rio Verde as it reflected the late afternoon sun.

On Sept. 21, 1972, the mine was sold to a Phoenix resident. In Sept. 1975, the owner received a letter from the Arizona Mining and Mineral Museum in appreciation for the receipt of 13 amethyst stones and crystals, some of which are still on display there.

On Mar. 3, 1977, the property was sold to Darrell E. Smith who operated it under the name Maricopa Mining Corporation. Unverified news stories at the time noted that Smith paid about $100,000 toward a purchase price of $350,000.

As early as November 1976, Smith was apparently planning the mine purchase. In that month he filed a "Notice of Intention to Operate on Public Land" with Tonto National Forest officials. He wrote a letter stating that the cost of the helicopter access was becoming prohibitive and that the only practical way of working the mine was with a heavy bulldozer. He further said that he had a D-8 Caterpillar positioned in a desert wash just 125 yards away from a spot where it could be "walked in" to the mine itself without again lowering the blade. He wanted to build a road over this short distance, and agreed to smooth over and to plant grass seed on any disturbed soil.

In June of 1977, permission was given to transport the D-8 for one time into the property and back out by the same route when the mine work was done. This letter from H. R. Nickless, Tonto Forest Ranger, specified that, "Under no conditions should the blade be dropped to move any soil or vegetation."

On Aug. 1, 1977, an angry letter from Mr. Nickless told Mr. Smith that Tonto Forest officials were aware that he had started a fire below his mine on the previous Saturday. Forest officers inspecting the damage also noticed that he had caused a significant amount of disturbance to National Forest land in moving the tractor to the mine. The road scar created by the bulldozer on the mountain below and to the left of the rock slope can still be seen in the late afternoon or just after a snowfall.

On Halloween Day in 1977, Ken Phillips and Art Bloyd, then-curator of the Mining and Mineral Museum, were at the mine site. They were evaluating the quality of crystals that had previously been discarded. As Phillips pointed out during a 1997 interview, "While the best crystals from there were outstanding, there was a significant amount of lesser grade material that was good enough to be profitably retrieved."

While Phillips and Bloyd were still there, Smith was operating his leased Caterpillar on the rock dumping area. It was steep and the material so loose that the D-8 overturned, sliding down the slope about 200 feet. Miraculously, Smith was unhurt but the tractor lost one of its tracks.

The tractor was leased from Empire Machinery of Mesa. They had to send a four-man crew to retrieve the machine. Orville Schubert, a retired Empire employee, remembers the scenic helicopter ride as repair parts and tools were flown to the site.

Others drove as far as possible and hiked on up the mountain. The track had to be repaired and remounted. Other repairs and maintenance were also required. Dynamite was used, with Tonto Forest approval, in rebuilding part of the trail to allow a safer route down the slope.

Two full days were needed to accomplish the task. The crew slept in the open at an elevation of about 7,100 feet on a very chilly night... "with only sleeping bags and a camp stove," Mr. Schubert said in a 1997 interview.

On the way out, a Tonto Forest Ranger was following closely to assure that no more damage would be done to the terrain and that no fire would be sparked. As the tractor was being brought off the mountain, it nearly overturned on three occasions. Mr. Schubert was the driver and he recalls, "I was plenty nervous-- I was sitting very lightly on that seat and ready to jump."

While these events were occurring, a letter was written from the Precious Minerals Corp. of New York City where Smith had sent samples for analysis. The expert there, Frank P. Jaeger, advised him that, "The color of Four Peaks does in fact, come up to African amethyst. Hang in there, Darrell, because I really think you have a winner." In a subsequent story for *Gems and Minerals* magazine, Jaeger says, "The amethyst produced at Four Peaks is distinctive....exquisite material, even the lilac colors have more 'zip' than the average."

Ironically, just as Mr. Smith was receiving these emphatic endorsements, the Tonto National Forest Service revoked his operating rights because of his damage to the wilderness outside the mine boundaries.

Ownership of the mine later reverted to the previous owner and the mine property is again for sale. This person wishes to remain anonymous. In return for this concession, he agreed to a recent interview and provided some of the details for this story.

Since the early 90's, no mining has taken place, due to the increasingly high price of helicopter access and the difficulty of gaining access to the remaining deposits.

The mine site is gated and trespassing is prohibited. Injuries to trespassers have occurred at the site and, on several occasions, hikers have become stranded. Persons have been arrested when they disregarded the posted notices. Four men were sentenced in Mesa on Feb. 4, 1969. One was put on probation for several years and prohibited from entering the Tonto National Forest in the Four Peaks vicinity. Forest Service helicopters occasionally monitor the site to prevent vandalism to this private property and to the wilderness area.

The valuable amethyst crystals have been removed except for those still locked deep inside the quartzite voids. Perhaps some day costs can be reduced or prices will rise enough for activity to again occur.

Until then we can but look and marvel at our proximity to a significant and unique site just 20 air miles away from Fountain Hills. A majestic purple mountain--in more ways than one!

POSTSCRIPT

Some chapters here were the result of original research. These were appealing to write and the most rewarding. This voyage of discovery has been both stimulating and slightly addictive.

Information was drawn from a variety of sources. Some of these disagreed on facts, dates, spelling and emphasis. After three or four generations, the trail is often faint. Choices had to be made. It's likely that an update five years from now would be amplified. That may serve as a goal, if the fates allow.

If *Verde Valley Lore* is enjoyable for a one-time "read," it will have served a purpose. If it causes some to periodically return for a review, that will be even more satisfying. If the stories make a few persons more attentive to the richness of this area's history or if it stimulates research of their own, then this author's objective will have been fulfilled.

R.M.

BIBLIOGRAPHY

Altshuler, Constance, *Chains of Command*, Az. Hist. Soc., Tucson, Az., 1981
Arizona Days and Ways, Dec. 29, 1959
Arizona Historical Foundations files, Hayden Library, Az. State Univ.
Arizona Room files, Phoenix Public Library, Phoenix, Az.
Barstad, Jan, *The Verde River Sheep Bridge*, G. A. Doyle, Phoenix, Az., 1988
Bourke, John, *On the Border With Crook*, Scribners, New York, N.Y.,1902
Carlson, Frances C., *A History of the Desert Foothills*, Encanto Press, Scottsdale, Az., 1988
Dancey, William S., *Archaeological Field Methods*, Burgess Publishing Co., Minneapolis, Mn., 1981
Dedera, Don, *A Little War Of Our Own*, Northland Press, Flagstaff, Az., 1988
Granger, Byrd H., *Arizona's Place Names*, Univ. of Az. Press, 1960
Hardt, Athia, Editor, *Arizona Waterline*, Salt River Project, undated
Horn, Tom, *Life of Tom Horn*, Crown Publishers, Inc., New York, N.Y., 1977
Krakel, Dean F., *The Saga of Tom Horn*, Univ. of Ne. Press, Powder River Publication, Laramie, Wy., 1954
Luhrs Reading Room Files, Hayden Library, Az. State Univ.
Merrill, Earl, *One Hundred Steps down Mesa's Past,* Lofgren Printing Co., Mesa, Az., 1975
Merrill, Earl, *One Hundred Yesterdays,* Lofgren Printing Co., Mesa, Az., 1972
Nabhan, Gary Paul, *Gathering the Desert*, Univ. of Az. Press, 1993
Reed, Bill, *The Last Bugle Call*, McLain Printing Co., Parsons, W. Va., 1977
Rogge, A. E., Raising Arizona's Dams, Univ. of Az. Press, Tucson, Az., 1995
Ruland-Thorne, Kate, *The Yavapai*, Thorne Enterprises, Inc., Sedona, Az.
Ruffner, Budge, *All Hell Needs is Water*, The Univ. of Az. Press, Tucson Az., 1972
Schreier, Jim, *Outpost in Apacheria*, Az. Hist. Soc., Tucson, Az., 1992
Stegner, Wallace, *Beyond the Hundredth Meridian*, Houghton Mifflin, Boston, Ma., 1954
Summerhayes, Martha, *Vanished Arizona*, Univ. of Ne. Press, Lincoln, Ne., 1979
Trimble, Marshall, *Roadside History of Arizona*, Mountain Press Publishing Co., Missoula, Mt., 1986
Trimble, Marshall, *Arizona Adventure*, Golden West Publishers, Phoenix, Az. 1982
Trimble, Marshall, *Arizona, A Cavalcade of History*, Treasure Chest Publications, Tucson, Az. 1989
Ward, Geoffrey C., *The Civil War*, Alfred Knopf, 1990
Waterstrat, Elaine, *Commanders and Chiefs*, Mount McDowell Press, Fountain Hills, Az., 1992
Zarbin, Earl, *Two Sides of the River*, Salt River Project, Phoenix, Az., 1997

INDEX

Numbers show title page of chapter where item can be found

A

A Little War of our Own	62,96
Adams, Jefferson Davis	90
Adams Mesa	90
Adams Ranch	62,90
African	140
Agua Fria River	103, 107
Alaska	31
Alfalfa In The Salt River Valley	103
Alma School Road	90
Al Sieber, Chief of Scouts	70
Amethyst	140
Anderson, Kenneth	90
Anglo	96
Antietam, Battle of	51
Apaches	1,35,39,45, 51,56,62, 70,75,96
Apache Lake	120
Apache Trail	62,70,120
Arbuckle Coffee	80
Archaeological Consulting Services	12
Archaeological Survey of Orme Reservoir	107
Arizona Amethyst Placer	140
Arizona Canal	124
Arizona Dam	124
Arizona Water Co.	124
Arizona Dark and Bloody Ground	96
Arizona Dept. Of Trans.	62,85,130
Arizona Dept. of Mines and Mineral Resources	140
Arizona Game and Fish Dept.	137
Arizona Historical Foundation	ii,35,56, 103
Arizona Hy. Dept.	130
Arizona Military Dept.	75
Arizona Miner	35,62,70
Arizona Mining Comm.	140
Arizona Mining and Mineral Museum	140
Arizona Place Names	103
Arizona Republic	107,116,130
Arizona Sheep Brdrs. and Wool Growers Ass'n.	96
Arizona State Capitol	107
Arizona State Univ.	16
Arizona Territory Brand Book	90
Arizona Territory	1,39,56,124
Arizona Territorial Gov.	35
Arizona Territorial Legislature	70
Arizona Wildlife Found.	107
ASU Wildlife Society	137
Arlington Cemetery	51
Arlington, Va.	31
Army of NE Va.	31
Army of the Potomac	39
Army of Rappahannock	31
Arts and Crafts Center	85
Asher, Frank	80
Asher Hills	80
Assryian	90
Atlantic & Pacific R.R.	96
Austin, Norman	107
Austin, Tx.	51
Australia	24
Avenue, 19th	80
Azatlan	12
Aztec	1,9
Aztlan	1
"Azul"	116

B

Bacchus	140
Baldwin, Mrs.	27
Baptist	27
Barr, Burton	107
Barstad, Jan	96
Bartlett, Bill	120
Bartlett Dam	80,96,107, 120
Bartlett Lake	80,120
Basque	96
Beaty, Aaron	56

INDEX

Beauregard, Gen. P.G.	31	California	31,39,45,56, 80,85,96
Beeline Highway	12,20,27,39, 56,62,80,90, 113,130,134	Camelback Mtn.	20
		Camp Eagle	62
Bell Road	90,103	Camp Carroll	62
Beltran/Espejo Expedition	116	Camp Miller	62
Bennett, Lt. Col.	35	Camp O'Connell	62
Bentonville, Ar.	130	Camp Reno	62,90,96,130
Bevens, Col.	45	Camp Verde	1,70,75, 80,90
Big Dry Wash, Battle of	51,70		
Bill Williams Mtns.	116	Cane Springs	96
Bisbee	39,70	Canouts, Valetta	107
Black Mountain	39	Canadian	31
Black River	116,120	Canyon Lake	96,120
Bloody Basin	96	CAP Canal	20,103,107
Bloyd, Art	140	Caribbean	85
Blue Point Bridge	12,96,134,137	Carefree	90,96
Boone, Daniel	70	Carino Canyon Homes	9
Bostwick, Todd	9	Carlisle School	27
Box Bar Ranch	90,96	Carlisle, Pa.	27
Boxer Rebellion	51	Carlock, Bob	85
Bradshaw Mtns.	1,70	Carr, Capt.	35
Brayton, Major	70	Carrizo Creek	116
Bridger, Jim	70	Carroll, James	45
Brooke, Bob	16,20	Carroll, Lt. J.C.	62
Brooks, Gabe	90	Carson, Kit	70
Brooklyn, N.Y.	27	Carter, Pres.	107
Brophy, Steve	85	Casa Grande	4
Brown, E.O.	90	Castro, Gov.	107
Brown Ranch	90	Caterpillar D-8	140
Buena Vista, Battle of	31	Catton, Bruce	31
Buffalo, N. Y.	39	Cavalliere Ranch	90
Bull Run, Battle of	31	Cave Creek	ii,39,70,103
Bureau of Indian Affairs	27,120	Cave Creek Road	39,103
Bureau of Land Mgt.	85	Central Arizona Project	107
Bureau of Reclamation	107	Chaffee, Capt.	45,70
Bush Highway	12,62,96,130, 134,137	Chaffee Parade Field	51
		Chaffee, M/M Truman	51
Bush, Harvey	130	Chandler, Az.	96
Butler, Carolina	107	Chavez, Lt. Col.	1
Butterfield Overland Mail and Stage	39	Chatauqua Co., NY.	39
		Cheyenne, Wyo.	75
C		Chicago	27
Cadillac Desert	51	Chicago Medical School	27
		Chilson, George W.	62
		China	51

INDEX

Chiricahua Indians	70,75	Dakota Territory	27
Chiricahua Mtns.	39,75	Davies, Flora Belle	80
Chisholm Trail	96	Davies, W.W. "Buzz"	80
Christopher Creek	70	Dedera, Don	62,96
Christopher, Isadore	70	Del Webb Construction Co.	113
Church of the Assumption	27	Democratic Party	39
Civil War	1,31,39,45, 51,62,70,90	Deming, New Mex.	103
		Dept. of Agriculture	85
Cliff Dam	107	Desert Land Act	45
Cline Ranch	90	Dept. of the Interior	124
Coconino National Forest	85	Dewey, Adm. George	137
Colonial period	12	Diana	140
Colorado	51,75	Dickens family	27
Colorado Crossing	39	Dobson, Dwayne	96
Colorado Plateau	16,96	Doubletree Ranch Rd.	103
Colorado River	85,107	Dowling, Annie	45
Columbus, Ohio	31	Dubois, Richard	62
Colville Agency	27	Dynamite Road	90
Commanders and Chiefs	35	**E**	
Committee to Save Ft. McDowell	107	Eagle Mountain	16
		East Coast	124
Confederacy	1	East Clear Creek	70
Confederate	31,39	East Verde River	70,116
Congress	27,45,85,107	Eldean, Fred & Margaret	85
Congressional Record	85	El Pueblo Blvd.	107
Conkey, Frank	103	"El Rio de los Reyes"	116
Cooke, Col. Phillip St. George	39	Empire Machinery Co.	140
		England	103
Cool Water	113	English	96
Coon Camp/Bluff	137	EPA	113
Coon's Point	137	Erie Canal	56
Corliss, Capt.	45	Europe	130
Coronado	96,116	Europeans	96,140
Cosmopolitan	75	Essex, Max	113
Crook, Gen.George	39,56,62,70, 75	Evans, Bob	85
		Evelin, Gertrude	140
Cruikshank, Alan	i,ii,85	**F**	
Curtis, Francis	80	Flagstaff	39,96
Custer, Gen.	39	Flagstaff Sheep Co.	96
Cuba	51	Florence, Az.	27,45,56
Cuba School	12	Forest Service	96,137,140
D		Forks of the River	137
DC Ranch	90	Forrest, Earl	96
Daggs Brothers	96	Fossil Creek	70

INDEX

Fountain Hills	1,9,12,16,20, 35,39,62,80, 85,90,107, 116,134,140	Gettysburg, Battle of	51,70
		Gila County	70,75
		Gila River	39,62
		Gila Valley	12
Fountain Hills High School	85	Gilbert, Az.	137
Fountain Hills Historical Society	85	Gilbert Road	12,56,113,134
		Glendenning, Fred	130
Fountain Hills Library	ii	Globe, Az.	39,62,70,75,80
Four Peaks	16,70,80,90 140	God of Wine	140
		Goldfield Mountains	16,134
Four Peaks Cattle Co.	85	Goldfield Ranch	90
Fowler, Benjamin	124	Goldwater, Barry	107
France	31	Graham, Tom	62
Friends of the Earth	107	Grand Canyon	16,70
French	62	Granite Reef Dam	20,113,124, 137
Fredricksburg, Battle of	51		
Ft. Apache	70,90,116	Grant, Gen. and Pres., U.S.	31,39,51
Ft. Brown, Tx.	39	Green Valley	62
Ft. Huachuca	51	Greer, Az.	96
Ft. Leavenworth, Ks.	39,51	Greek	4,134,140
Ft. McDowell	1,12,27,31, 35,39,45,51, 56,62,70,75, 80,90,130	Gulf of California	62
		H	
		Hancock, William	35
		Handle, Paul	56
Ft. McDowell Indians	107	Hansbrough-Newlands Act	124
Ft. McDowell Reservation	12,27,31,80, 90,107	Hart Highway, James	130
		Hassayampa River	1
Ft. Riley, Ks.	51	Havana, Cuba	51
Ft. Stevenson	27	Hayden, Charles	56
Ft. Utah	56	Hayden's Ferry	56
Ft. Whipple	1,39,56	Hayden Library	ii
Ft. Worth	80	Hayden, Rep. Carl	45
G		Hayden Road	80
Gainey, Dan	130	Hayden, Sen. Carl	107
Gainey Ranch	130	Heard, Dwight B	124
Galesburg, Il.	27	Heard, John, Sr.	75
Gems and Minerals	140	Heber, Az.	96
Geneva U.N. Conference	107	Heber-Reno Driveway	96
Gentile, Carlos	27	Herculaneum	134
Geology of the Lower Verde Valley	16	Herberger, Bob	130
		Higby, Deputy Sheriff	75
German	70,140	Hispanic	96,124
Germany's Rhineland	70	Hoff, Julie	62
Geronimo	70,75	Hohokam	i,4,9,12,24,31, 35,45,90,103, 124
Geronimo Head Formation	134		

INDEX

Hood, Hiawatha	107
Horn, Tom	51
Horne Road	56
Horse Mesa Dam	120
Horseshoe Dam	96,103,107, 120
Horseshoe Lake	90,120
House of Amethyst	140
Hudson Reservoir and Canal Co.	124
Hughes, Bernard	90
Humboldt Mountain	20
Hurlbut, Hank & Violet	85

I

Indian Agents	51
Indian Bend Wash	103
Indian School Road	80
Invergordon Road	103
Italy	134
Ireland	45
Iverson, Peter	27

J

Jacobs, M., Gen'l. Mdse.	80
Jackson, Thomas J.	39
Jackson, "Stonewall"	39
Jaeger, Frank P.	140
Jamaica ginger	62
Jerome, Az.	70
Jones, Daniel W.	56
Jones, Rollin	137
Juchem, Louis and Rudolf	140
Juniper Mountains	116

K

KA Ranch	90
Kansas	51
Kansas City	80
Keller, Marie	27
Kendall, Lt. H. N.	45,51

L

La Escuela Cuba	12
La Paz, Az.	1
Lake Havasu City	85
Laramide stage	16
Last Bugle Call	35
Lawton, Gen.	51
Lee, Robert E.	31
Lehi Boy Scouts	137
Lehi party	56,124
Lehi Road	56
Libby Prison	45
Lincoln, Pres. Abraham	31
Loco Campaign	70
London Bridge	85
Lone Pine Saddle	90
Longhorn cattle	90
Lousley Hill	16
Los Angeles	51,140
Los Angeles Public Works	51
Luhrs Reading Room	ii
Lynn pasture	80
Lyon, Oscar	130

M

Manila Bay	137
Maricopa Co., Az	80,85,90,124, 130
Maricopa Co. Audubon Society	107
Maricopa Co. Bd. of Supervisors	130
Maricopa Mining Corp.	140
Maricopa Indians	27
Maricopa Wells, Az.	56
Marin Co., Ca.	85
Maryville Amateur Troupe	56
Maryville Crossing	56
Maryville *Hornet*	56
Mason, Dorothy	ii
Mason, Gen. John S.	31
Mason, Marty	ii
Masonic Lodge	1
Massachusetts	45
Maverick Mountain	80
Maxwell, George	124
Mayo Clinic	9,85
Mazatzal Mtns.	16,39,62,80, 90,96,140
Mazatzal Wilderness	96
MacArthur, Maj. Gen. Arthur	51

INDEX

MacArthur, Douglas	51	Montezuma Health Center	27
McClellan, Gen.	31	Moore, Lynn	90
McClintock, Charles E.	124	Moore, W. W.	80
McConville, Mac	ii	Morenci, Az.	120
McCormick, Richard	35	Mormon	56,124
McCulloch Corporation	85,107	Mormon Battalion	39
McDaniels, Jim	140	Mormon Flat Dam	120
McDowell Crossing	56	Mt. McDowell	16,20
McDowell, Gen. Irvin	35		
McDowell Mountains	i,16,20,31,85, 90,103	**N**	
		Nan-tia-tish	70
McDowell Mtn. Road	39	Nat'l. Hist.Landmark	120
McDowell Mtn. Park	20,39,85,90	Nat'l Register of Hist. Places	96
McDowell-Reno Road	70	Nat'l. Wildlife Society	107
McDowell Reservation	27,80	Native Americans	24,27,31,56, 96,107
McDowell Road	12,31,56, 130,134	Navajos	96
		Needle Rock	16,39,45,70,90
McMillanville, Az.	70	New England	31,62
Merrill, Earl	56,124,137	New Mexico	4,51
Mesa	ii,56,62,70, 120,124,130, 137,140	New Mexico Territory	1,116
		New River	9
		New York City	27,140
Mesa Boy Scouts	56	*New York Herald*	51
Mesa Library	ii	Nevada	27
Mesa Tribune	56,96,124,137	Nickell family	75
Mesa Verde	4	Nickell, Willie	75
Mexican border	39	Nickless, H.R.	140
Mexico	1,4,70,75,90	North America	107,120
Mexican War	31	North Dakota	103
Mexican	45,62,85	Northeast Arizona	96
Miami, Az.	62	Northeast United States	103
Micek, John and Nancy	45	Northern Arizona	96
Military Road	39	Northland Research	12
Miller family	75	Northwestern University	27
Mills, William	62	**O**	
Minie', Capt. Claude	62	O'Connell, Major John	62
Mineralogical Record	140	Ochoa Ranch	90
Mineralogy in Arizona	140	Office of Indian Affairs	27
Minneapolis, Mn.	70	Ohio Cavalry, 6th	51
Missouri	75	Ohmart, Dr. Robert	107
Mogollon Plateau	16	Oklahoma	51
Mogollon Rim	62,70,96	Omaha	80
Monroy, Pancho	90	"Onk Akimel"	116
Montezuma, Carlos	27	Orange Patch	56
Montezuma, Dr. Carlos	130	Oregon	39

INDEX

Orme Dam	85,116	Pima Indians	27,56,70,116
Orme, John P.	107,124	Pinal Apaches	56
Orwell, Ohio	51	Pinkerton Agency	75
Ottinger, Dr. Millard	85	Pinnacle West	137
"Out of Africa"	113	Pittsburg, Ks.	130
Owatonna, Mn.	130	Pittsburg Business College	130
P		Plan 6	107
P-Bar Ranch	90,96	Pleasant Valley Trail	62
Pacific Ocean	4,12	Pleasant Valley War	62,75,96
Page Land & Cattle Co.	80,85,90,130	Plinian Deposits	134
Papago Buttes	16,20	Pliny The Elder	134
Paradise Valley	103	Pliny The Younger	134
Paradise Valley Inn	85	Point Reyes Nat'l. Seashore	85
Paradise Valley Water Co.	80	Pompeii	134
Parke, Lt. John G.	39	Pope, Clifford, Jr.	16
Pavilions Shopping Center	80	Pope, Gen. John	31
Payson, Az.	62,70,116,130	Poston, Charles	1
Payson Hospital	130	Powderhorn Ranch	90
Pederson, Mark	96	Pratt, Lorne	85
Pedro, Chief	75	Pre-Cambrian period	16
Peking, China	51	Precious Minerals Corp.	140
Pemberton Ranch	90	Prescott	1,35,39,45,
Peninsula Campaign	51		56,62,70,75
Pennsylvania	70,137	Presidio	31,39
Phelps Dodge Corp.	120	Priestly, John	96
Philadelphia	62	"Prieto"	116
Philadelphia Times	75	Pueblo Grande	12
Phillipine Islands	51,137	**R**	
Phillips, Ken	140	Raymond, Dr.	96
Phoenician	90	Read, Frank	45
Phoenix	ii,9,27,35,39,	Read, Mary	85
	45,56,70,75,	Reavis, Mr.	45
	80,85,90,96,	Red Mountain	16,20,56,113
	103,107,113,		124,134
	120,124,130,	Red Mountain Trap and	
	140	Skeet	56
Phoenix Chamber of		Red Point Bridge	96
Commerce	116	Reed, Bill	35
Phoenix Daily Herald	103,124	Reigle, Dallas	116
Phoenix Gazette	124,130	Reno, Maj. Gen. Jesse	62
Phoenix Library	ii	Reno Pass	62
Phoenix-Payson Highway	130	Republican Party	130
Phoenix Water Dept.	113	Reynolds Aluminum	130
Picket Post Butte	39	Rhodes, Rep. John	107
"Pig Farm"	90	Richmond, Va.	45

INDEX

"Rio Alamos"	116	Salt River/Pima Reservation	27
"Rio Compuesto"	116	Salt River Project	ii,103,116, 120,124
"Rio de la Assuncion"	116		
"Rio de las Balsas"	116	Salt River Water User's Association	107,124
"Rio Salinas"	116		
"Rio Verde"	1,35,56	Salt River Valley	9,12,39,96,103, 107,116,124
Rio Verde	1,12,16,20, 80,140		
		San Antonio	39
Rio Verde Canal Co.	103,124	San Carlos Agency	75
Rio Verde Drive	39,90	San Carlos Reservation	70,120
Rio Verde Ranch	45	San Diego	39
Roadside History of Arizona	1	San Francisco	31,35,39,45
Robbins, Dick	85	"San Francisco"	116
Robinson, Jerry	80	San Gabriel Valley	39
Rock Hobby Shop	140	Santa Fe	39,75
Rogers, Roy	113	San Juan Hill	75
Romanian/American	27	Santa Lucia Corp.	85
Romo Ranch	62,90	Santa Lucia Island	85
Roosevelt, Az.	70	Santorini	134
Roosevelt Dam	27,62,70,107, 120,124	Sawik Mountain	56
		Schieffelin, Ed	75
Roosevelt Lake	116,120	Schnering, Philip	1
Roosevelt, Lt. Col.	75	Schubert, Orville	140
Roosevelt, Pres. Theodore	51,120,124	Scientific Archaeological Services	12
Rough Riders	75		
Rowe, Thomas	56	Scott, Winfield	31
Rowe, William	56	Scottsdale	9,16,80,90, 103,130,140
Rudd, Rep. Eldon	107		
Rusling, Brig. Gen.	35	Scottsdale Community College	62
Ryan, Will	80		
S		Scottsdale Road	103,130
Saddleback Mountain	9,16	Sea of Cortez	4
Safford, Gov.	39	Sears--Club--Chalk Mtn.	90
Saguaro Blvd.	107	Sears-Kay Ranch	90
Saguaro Lake	120,130,134	Seven Springs	90,96
"Salado"	1,116	Shaffer, Prof. Gary	62
Salado Indians	12	Sharpe's ammunition	62
Salt Lake City	56	Shaw, Adrian	85
Salt River	1,12,20,24, 35,56,62,85, 90,96,103, 107,113,116, 120,124,134, 137	Shea Blvd.	9,16,27,85, 103,130
		Shea Homes	9
		Sheep Crossing	62
		Sheep Springs Sheep Co.	96
		Sheldon, Augustus C.	103
Salt River Canyon	116	Sheridan, Gen.	39
Salt River/Pima Indians	130	Shortell, Thomas	56

INDEX

Shoshone Agency	27		Summerhayes, Capt.	45
Siberian	140		Summerhayes, Martha	45,56
Sieber, Al	75		Sunflower, Az.	62
Sierra Nevada Mtns.	51		Superstition Wilderness	16,134
Sinagua Indians	12		Sutton, Phon , Jr.	137
Sirrine, Roy	137		Swilling, Jack	35,124
Sitgreaves National Forest	85		Sycamore Creek	62,70,90,96
Sky Harbor Airport	12		Symonds, Maj.	103
Smith, Darrell E.	140		**T**	
Smith, Lt.	39		Taliesin West	90
Smithsonian Museum	107		Tangle Creek	96
Soil Systems, Inc.	12		Tempe	45,56
Soldiers Nat'l Cemetery	31		Tempe Democrats	107
Sons of the Pioneers	113		Tewksburys	96
South America	62		Tewksbury, Ed	62
Southeast Asia	24		Texas	45,51,90,96
Southwest Archaeological Ass'n.	62		Texas Trail	96
South Sea Islands	24		"The Killing of the Captain"	75
Southside Gas and Electric Co.	137		*The Life of Tom Horn*	75
			The Times of Fountain Hills	i,ii,85
Spain	90		Thomas Road	113
Spanish	1,56,75,90,116, 134,137,140		Thrapp, Dan	70
			Toddy Mountain	62
Spanish-American War	51,75,137		Tombstone	75
Spencer cartridges	62		*Tombstone Weekly Epitaph*	39
St. Lucia	85		Tonto Apaches	56,70
Stade, Andrew	103		Tonto Basin	39,62,90,96
Standard Oil	137		Tonto National Forest	ii,80,90,96, 137,140
Stanton, Sec. of War	51		Tonto Creek	62,70,116,124
Steadman, William	27		Tonto Verde	1,12,20,80
Stewart Mountain Dam	12,107,120,134		"Trail of Tears"	107
Stoneman, Gen. George	31,70		Toomey, Elijah	56
Stoneman Grade	39		Trimble, Marshall	1
Stoneman Lake	39		Tsosie, Boyd and Richard	85
Stoneman Military Road	i,51,56		Tucson	1,20,107
Stoneman's Raid	51		Tucson *Arizona Citizen*	56
Storer, Al and Cecile	140		Tucson Audubon Society	107
Strawberry, Az.	51		**U**	
Street, 56th	103		Underwood, Mr.	56
Street, 64th	113		Union Army	31,39,45
Street, 136th	39,90		University of Arizona	24
Street, 140th	16		University of Illinois	27
Stuart, Jeb	39		Urbana, Il.	27
Stute, Jim	62		U.S. Census Bureau	103
Sugarloaf Mountain	62,96		U.S. Senate	107

INDEX

U.S. Geological Survey	116
U.S. Topographical Engineers	39
Usery Mountains	16,134
Usery Park	134
Usery Pass	96,134
Utah	51,120

V

"Valley of the Sun"	116
Vanished Arizona	45,56
Velasco, Benjamin	12
Velasco, Ditch	12
Verde River	i,1,12,16,24, 27,31,39,45, 51,56,62,70, 80,85,90,96, 103,107,113, 116,120,137
Verde River Sheep Bridge	96
Verde Valley	ii,1,4,9,12,16, 35,90,96,107, 116,134
Vesuvius	134

W

Waddell Dam	107
Wallace, Lt. Col.	62
Wall Street Journal	107
War Dept.	45
Washington	27
Washington, D.C.	31,39,45,107, 124
Wassaja	27,130
Waterstrat, Elaine	35
Water Users Site	12
Watt, James	103
Watt, James, Sec. of Interior	107
Weaver's Needle	16
West Weldon St.	75
Wells Fargo	80
West Coast	62
West Point	31,39,51
Western United States	39,124
Westwing Mountains	9
White, Annie	45
White Ditch	45
White, Patrick	45,51
White Mountains	116
White River	116
Whitlow, Allen & Charles	56
Whitlow, Charles, Jr.	56
Whitlow Rodeo Grounds	56
Whitlow Crossing	56
Whitlow, Mary Elizabeth	56
Whitney, John	90
Wickenburg, Az.	39,56,90
Williams Field	56
Wilson, J.J.	56
Wilson, Pres.	80
Wind Cave Trail	134
Winkelman, Az.	75
Witzeman, Dr. Robert	107
Wood, C.V., Jr.	85
Wood, Col. Leonard	75
World War I	75
World War II	113,130
Wright, Frank Lloyd	90
Wyoming	45,75
Wyoming Stock Owner's Association	75
Wyoming Supreme Court	75

X

X-2 Ranch	90

Y

Yavapai Indians	27,107
Yavapai County	75
Young, Az.	62,75
Young Republicans	107
Yucatan	4
Yuma	39,45,56

Z

Zulick, Governor	45
Zuni, N. Mex.	1

THE AUTHOR

Robert Mason was reared on a southern Kansas farm. After two years at Wichita State University, he served in the Army Air Force, then graduated from Kansas State University.

He retired in 1983 following a 34-year career with Minneapolis, Minnesota-based Cargill, Inc. He and his wife reside in Rio Verde, Arizona where his activities include community affairs, hiking, golf, tennis, genealogy, archaeology and bridge